GREEN
EDITION

Bob Miller's
Math *for the*
TABE LEVEL A

D1708113

Test of Adult Basic Education

All the Math You Need
for a Higher Score

By Bob Miller

Research & Education Association
Visit our website at: *www.rea.com*

Planet Friendly Publishing
✔ Made in the United States
✔ Printed on Recycled Paper
  Text: 10%   Cover: 10%
Learn more: www.greenedition.org

At REA we're committed to producing books in an Earth-friendly manner and to helping our customers make greener choices.

Manufacturing books in the United States ensures compliance with strict environmental laws and eliminates the need for international freight shipping, a major contributor to global air pollution.

And printing on recycled paper helps minimize our consumption of trees, water and fossil fuels. This book was printed on paper made with **10% post-consumer waste**. According to the Environmental Paper Network's Paper Calculator, by using this innovative paper instead of conventional papers, we achieved the following environmental benefits:

Trees Saved: 4 • Air Emissions Eliminated: 832 pounds
Water Saved: 787 gallons • Solid Waste Eliminated: 246 pounds

Courier Corporation, the manufacturer of this book, owns the Green Edition Trademark.
For more information on our environmental practices, please visit us online at **www.rea.com/green**

Research & Education Association
61 Ethel Road West
Piscataway, New Jersey 08854
E-mail: info@rea.com

BOB MILLER'S
Math for the TABE Level A

Published 2013
Copyright © 2010 by Research & Education Association, Inc.
All rights reserved. No part of this book may be reproduced in any form without permission of the publisher.

Printed in the United States of America

Library of Congress Control Number 2008944122

ISBN-13: 978-0-7386-0554-8
ISBN-10: 0-7386-0554-9

REA® is a registered trademark of
Research & Education Association, Inc.

TABLE OF CONTENTS

ACKNOWLEDGMENTS

I have many people to thank.

I thank my wife, Marlene, who makes life worth living, who is truly the wind under my wings.

I thank the rest of my family: children Sheryl and Eric and their spouses Glenn and Wanda (who are also like my children); grandchildren Kira, Evan, Sean, Sarah, and Ethan; my brother Jerry; and my parents, Cele and Lee; and my in-law parents, Edith and Siebeth.

I thank Larry Kling and Michael Reynolds for making this book possible.

I thank Martin Levine for making my whole writing career possible.

I have been negligent in thanking my great math teachers of the past. I thank Mr. Douglas Heagle, Mr. Alexander Lasaka, Mr. Joseph Joerg, and Ms Arloeen Griswold, the best math teacher I ever had, of George W. Hewlett High School; Ms. Helen Bowker of Woodmere Junior High; and Professor Pinchus Mendelssohn and Professor George Bachman of Polytechnic University. The death of Professor Bachman was an extraordinary loss to our country. In a country that produces too few advanced degrees in math, every year two or three of his students would receive a Ph.D. in math, with more receiving their M.S. His teaching and writings were clear and memorable. He wrote four books and numerous papers on subjects that had never been written about or had been written about so poorly that nobody could understand the material.

As usual, the last three thanks go to three terrific people: a great friend, Gary Pitkofsky; another terrific friend and fellow lecturer, David Schwinger; and my cousin, Keith Robin Ellis, the sharer of our dreams.

Bob Miller

DEDICATION

*To my wife Marlene. I dedicate this book and everything else I ever do to you.
I love you very, very much.*

BIOGRAPHY

I received my B.S. in the Unified Honors Program sponsored by the Ford Foundation and my M.S. in math from Polytechnic University. After the first class I taught, as a substitute for a full professor, one student said to another upon leaving the classroom, "At least we have someone who can teach the stuff." I was hooked forever on teaching. Since then, I have taught at C.U.N.Y., Westfield State College, Rutgers, and Poly. No matter how I feel, I always feel a lot better when I teach. I always feel great when students tell me they used to hate math or couldn't do math and now they like it more and can do it better.

My main blessing is my family. I have a fantastic wife in Marlene. My kids are wonderful: daughter Sheryl, son Eric, son-in-law Glenn, and daughter-in-law Wanda. My grandchildren are terrific: Kira, Evan, Sean, Sarah, and Ethan. My hobbies are golf, bowling, bridge, crossword puzzles, and Sudoku. My ultimate goals are to write a book to help parents teach their kids math, a high school text that will advance our kids' math abilities, and a calculus text students can actually understand.

To me, teaching is always a great joy. I hope that I can give some of that joy to you. I do know this book will help you know what you need.

Good luck!!!!!

OTHER BOOKS

Bob Miller's Math Prep for the Compass Exam

Bob Miller's Math for the Accuplacer

Bob Miller's Math for the ACT

Bob Miller's Math for the New GRE

Bob Miller's Math for the GMAT

Bob Miller's Basic Math and Pre-Algebra for the Clueless, Second Edition

Bob Miller's Algebra for the Clueless, Second Edition

Bob Miller's Geometry for the Clueless, Second Edition

Bob Miller's Math SAT for the Clueless, Second Edition

Bob Miller's Pre-Calc with Trig for the Clueless, Third Edition

Bob Miller's High School Calc for the Clueless

Bob Miller's Calc 1 for the Clueless, Second Edition

Bob Miller's Calc 2 for the Clueless, Second Edition

Bob Miller's Calc 3 for the Clueless

ABOUT RESEARCH & EDUCATION ASSOCIATION

Founded in 1959, Research & Education Association (REA) is dedicated to publishing the finest and most effective educational materials—including software, study guides, and test preps—for students in middle school, high school, college, graduate school, and beyond.

REA's test preparation series includes books and software for all academic levels in almost all disciplines. REA publishes test preps for students who have not yet entered high school, as well as high school students preparing to enter college. Students from countries around the world seeking to attend college in the United States will find the assistance they need in REA's publications. For college students seeking advanced degrees, REA publishes test preps for many major graduate school admission examinations in a wide variety of disciplines, including engineering, law, and medicine. Students at every level, in every field, with every ambition can find what they are looking for among REA's publications.

REA's publications and educational materials are highly regarded and continually receive an unprecedented amount of praise from professionals, instructors, librarians, parents, and students. Our authors are as diverse as the subject matter represented in the books we publish. They are well known in their respective disciplines and serve on the faculties of prestigious colleges and universities throughout the United States and Canada.

Today, REA's wide-ranging catalog is a leading resource for teachers, students, and professionals.

We invite you to visit us at *www.rea.com* to find out how "REA is making the world smarter."

REA ACKNOWLEDGMENTS

In addition to our author, we would like to thank Larry B. Kling, Vice President, Editorial, for his overall direction; Pam Weston, Vice President, Publishing, for setting the quality standards for production integrity and managing the publication to completion; Michael Reynolds, Managing Editor, for project management; Mel Friedman, Lead Mathematics Editor, for proofreading; Rachel DiMatteo, Graphic Designer, for designing this book; Christine Saul, Senior Graphic Artist, for designing our cover; and Matrix Publishing Services for typesetting this edition. Photo by Eric L. Miller.

A NOTE ON CALCULATORS

Calculators are permitted on the second part of the exam.

TO THE STUDENT

Congratulations to you!!!! You are taking the first step toward getting your GED. Your immediate goal is to get your diploma so that you can earn more money for yourself and your family. However, you may find greater rewards in learning things you never thought you could.

You might think you cannot learn math. Wrong! Because of the way math is taught today, almost all students think that they can't learn math or that they are stupid. I live in a community in which some brilliant students take calculus in high school but they don't know all of their basic arithmetic or basic algebra. When students come to me, many think it's their fault they can't learn. That's wrong! In fact, I have often said that if I were to take math today, I'm not sure I could learn it, and I really, really know this stuff!

Nearly every student, good or not, high level or not, has the same problems. See if this is also you. Students generally know their decimals pretty well, have trouble with fractions, and are really bad with percentages (I have a neat way of showing them to you!). Algebra students usually know how to solve basic equations, but after that, many of the basics are unclear.

This book will change all this. You will learn the skills necessary for this test and why what you learn is true (very important for learning). The book has practice problems to help you improve your skill.

The other part you need to know is to how to read a math book. I was never taught this, and I have a Masters degree in math. It is exactly the opposite of reading a book for English, where the goal is to read fairly quickly and still understand the book. The way to read a math book is sl-o-o-o-o-o-o-wly, line by line. When there are examples, you have to write them and go over them until you understand them. Some topics will take longer than others to learn. However, your overall speed at learning will get faster as you get further into the book. At the end of the book, you will be so much better than when you started, you won't believe it! Many of my students have discovered this.

So let's get going!

Bob Miller

CHAPTER 1: *The Basics*

"*All math begins with whole numbers. Master them and you will begin to speak the language of math.*"

At the beginning of each topic in math, there are lots of new words. These are necessary. You know most of these, but some might be new to you.

NUMBERS

Counting Numbers (sometimes called the **natural numbers**): 1, 2, 3, 4, . . .

The three dots at the end mean the numbers go on forever.

Whole numbers: 0, 1, 2, 3, 4, . . .

Note *The word "number" does not necessarily mean whole number. It could be a fraction or decimal.*

Example 1: On a **line graph** or **number line**, graph the numbers 2, 4, 6, 9.

Solution: Draw a line. Mark off the number line in equal lengths. Locate one number less than the smallest number and one number larger than the largest, if possible. Put in the 0 if reasonable.

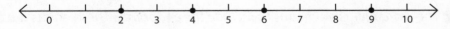

To find counting numbers that are multiples of 3, multiply each whole number by 3: 0(3), 1(3), 2(3), 3(3), 4(3), . . . , or 0, 3, 6, 9, 12, . . .

Notes

1. Notice the pattern here. The difference between the numbers is 3. Later in the book we will do more on patterns.

2. Sometimes the test will just say "multiples of 3."

3. Remember that the three dots at the end mean the pattern goes on forever.

4. Multiplication is shown in different ways. Three times four can be written 3(4), (3)(4), (3)4, 3 * 4, or 3 × 4. Algebra usually doesn't use the symbol × for multiplication; however, at this point, you will still see it a lot!

Example 2: Graph all whole number multiples of 3.

Solution:

0, 3, 6, 9, 12, . . .

Note *The arrows mean the number pattern continues forever.*

Even Whole Numbers: 0, 2, 4, 6, . . . This is similar to the case for counting numbers that are multiples of 3. Therefore, even whole numbers are sometimes called multiplies of two. Notice that in this pattern, the difference between each number is 2.

Odd Whole Numbers: 1, 3, 5, 7, . . . Here the difference between the numbers is also 2, but the first number is 1.

Example 3: Graph all multiples of 5 between 40 and 70.

Solution:

Notes

1. It is convenient to make the intervals on the graph multiples of 5.

2. The word **between** means the end numbers are *not* included.

3. It is *not* convenient here to graph the zero. A graph can be any interval that makes sense.

Example 4: Graph all the multiples of 4 between 40 and 60, inclusive.

Solution:

Note *The word **inclusive** means to include the endpoints. These points have filled-in circles.*

If c is to the right of d on the number line, we say $c > d$, read as "c is greater than d." Therefore, $8 > 5$ because 8 is to the right of 5 on the number line.

If d is to the left of c on the number line, we say $d < c$. Therefore, $2 < 5$ because 2 is to the left of 5 on the number line.

$c > d$ is the same as $d < c$. $9 > 6$ is the same as $6 < 9$.

Because 3 * 4 = 12, 3 and 4 are said to be **factors** or **divisors** of 12, and 12 is both a **multiple** of 3 (3, 6, 9, 12, 15, . . .) and a **multiple** of 4 (4, 8, 12, 16, . . .).

A **prime** number is a positive integer with exactly two distinct factors, itself and 1.

1 is not considered a prime, since only 1 * 1 = 1.

It is a good idea to learn the first eight primes: 2, 3, 5, 7, 11, 13, 17, and 19.

Example 5:   Find all the primes between 70 and 80.

Solution: 71, 73, 79. How do we find these primes easily? The only even prime is 2, so we only have to check the odd numbers, 71, 73, 75, 77, and 79. 75 is not a prime because it is ends in a 5 (any number that ends in a 0 or 5 is divisible by 5). 77 is not a prime because it is divisible by 7. To see if the other three are prime, for any number less than 100 you have to divide by the primes 2, 3, 5, and 7 only. You will quickly find they are primes.

The number 4 has more than two factors: 1, 2, and 4. Numbers with more than two factors are called **composites**.

Example 6:   Write all the factors of 28.

Solution: 1, 2, 4, 7, 14, and 28.

Note   *28 is a **perfect** number, which means the number equals the sum of all its factors (less than the number itself). 1 + 2 + 4 + 7 + 14 = 28.*

Product is the answer in multiplication; **quotient** is the answer in division; **sum** is the answer in addition; and **difference** is the answer in subtraction.

There are three ways to show division: $12 \div 3$, 12/3, and $3\overline{)12}$. In algebra, almost exclusively, we use the fraction. On this test, we need to recognize all three. In any case, 12/3 = 4 because 3(4) = 12.

Before we go on, let's talk about the troublesome numbers. No, no, no—I don't mean 12,987,564,957. I mean **zero**. It causes more trouble than any other number. Here are the rules for zero:

Rule 1: $0 + a = a + 0 = a$. If you add zero to a number, you get that number. $0 + 6 = 6 + 0 = 6$.

Rule 2: $a(0) = 0$. Any number multiplied by 0 is 0; $(8)(0) = 0$.

Rule 3: Division with 0 is the most difficult. *You cannot divide by 0.* Let us show why. $\frac{7}{0}$ cannot have an answer. If the answer were *c*, this would mean $0(c) = 7$; however, the second rule tells us that $0(c) = 0$. Therefore, $0(c) = 7$ has no answer for a value of *c*. So you cannot divide by 0.

However, you can divide a number into 0: $\frac{0}{4} = 0$ because $0 = 4(0)$.

EXPONENTS (POWERS)

If we write x^a, the *x* is the **base** and the *a* is the **exponent** or **power**. Calculating a number with an exponent, also called "raising a number to a power," means writing the number as many times as the power, and then multiplying. So $x^4 = x * x * x * x$.

Note *You are performing multiplication one less time than the power.* x^4 *involves only three multiplications, but there are four factors.*

1. $b = b^1$, which is read as "*b* to the first power." The 1 is understood. Thus, $7 = 7^1$.

2. $s^2 = s(s)$ is read as "*s* squared" or "*s* to the second power"; so 9^2 is read as "9 squared," and equals $9 * 9 = 81$.

3. x^3 is read as "*x* cubed" or "*x* to the third power"; x^3 means $(x)(x)(x)$. So $4^3 = 4 * 4 * 4$. This is read as "4 to the third power" or "4 cubed." It equals 64.

4. $N^4 = N * N * N * N$, and is read as "*N* to the fourth power." Notice that there are four factors. Thus, $5^4 = 5 * 5 * 5 * 5 = 625$. This is read "5 to the fourth power."

The TABE expects you to know the following common powers, especially on the sections for which you cannot use your calculator. It would pay to memorize the ones you do not know already:

$0^2 = 0$	$1^2 = 1$	$2^2 = 4$	$3^2 = 9$	$4^2 = 16$	$5^2 = 25$
$6^2 = 36$	$7^2 = 49$	$8^2 = 64$	$9^2 = 81$	$10^2 = 100$	
$11^2 = 121$	$12^2 = 144$	$13^2 = 169$	$14^2 = 196$	$15^2 = 225$	
$1^3 = 1$	$2^3 = 8$	$3^3 = 27$	$4^3 = 64$	$5^3 = 125$	
$6^3 = 216$	$7^3 = 343$	$8^3 = 512$	$9^3 = 729$	$10^3 = 1000$	
$1^4 = 1$	$2^4 = 16$	$3^4 = 81$	$4^4 = 256$	$5^4 = 625$	

Rule 1 for exponents: If you are multiplying numbers with the same bases, add the exponents and leave the base alone!!

Example 7: $2^5 * 2^3 =$

Solution: The answer is 2^8 if the exponential form is asked for; it is 256 otherwise. Why should you believe me? Let me show you why: $2^5 * 2^3 = (2 * 2 * 2 * 2 * 2)(2 * 2 * 2) = 2^8$ because there are eight 2's being multiplied!

Rule 2 for exponents: If you are dividing numbers with the same bases, subtract the exponents, and leave the base alone.

Example 8: $\dfrac{3^6}{3^4} =$

Solution: The answer is 3^2 if the exponential form is asked for; it is 9 otherwise. Again, why should you believe me?!

$$\frac{3^6}{3^4} = \frac{3 \times 3 \times 3 \times 3 \times 3 \times 3}{3 \times 3 \times 3 \times 3} = 3^2 = 9$$ because four of the 3's on the top will cancel out the four 3's on the bottom.

We will do more exponential problems throughout the book.

ORDER OF OPERATIONS

In doing a problem like this, $4 + 5 * 6$, order of operations tells us whether to multiply or add first.

Order of operations:

1. Do parentheses, brackets, or braces, inside ones first.

2. Do the tops and bottoms of fractions.

3. Exponents are next.

4. Do multiplications and divisions, left to right as they occur.

5. The last step is adding and subtracting. Left to right is the safest way for many problems.

Note *( ) are called parentheses (singular: parenthesis); [ ] are called brackets; { } are called braces.*

Example 9:

Problems	Solutions
a. $4 + 5 * 6$	$4 + 30 = 34$
b. $(4 + 5) * 6$	$(9)(6) = 54$
c. $1000 \div 2 * 4$	$(500)(4) = 2000$
d. $1000 \div (2 * 4)$	$1000 \div 8 = 125$
e. $4[3 + 2(5 - 1)]$	$4[3 + 2(4)] = 4[3 + 8] = 4(11) = 44$
f. $\dfrac{3^4 - 1^{10}}{4 + 12 \times 3}$	$\dfrac{81 - 1}{4 + 36} = \dfrac{80}{40} = 2$

Note *The parentheses make a big difference in parts c and d.*

Here are some other facts about odd and even numbers you may need to know.

1.   The sum of two even integers is even.

2.   The sum of two odd integers is even.

3.   The sum of an even and an odd is odd.

4.   The product of two evens is an even.

5.   The product of two odds is odd.

6.   The product of an even and an odd is an even.

7.   If n is even, n^2 is even. If n^2 is even and n is a whole number, then n is even.

8.   If n is odd, n^2 is odd. If n^2 is odd and n is a whole number, then n is odd.

You should try these facts on some numbers to convince yourself they are true.

SQUARE ROOTS

The one math symbol that everyone seems to like is the square root. How else can you explain the square root key on a business calculator that no one ever uses?

The **square root** of 9, written $\sqrt{9} = 3$ because $3 * 3 = 3^2 = 9$.

Because the TABE has questions for which you cannot use a calculator, you must know certain square roots.

$$\sqrt{1} = 1 \quad \sqrt{4} = 2 \quad \sqrt{9} = 3 \quad \sqrt{16} = 4 \quad \sqrt{25} = 5$$
$$\sqrt{36} = 6 \quad \sqrt{49} = 7 \quad \sqrt{64} = 8 \quad \sqrt{81} = 9 \quad \sqrt{100} = 10$$

Note *These are the opposites of the square powers we discussed earlier.*

Example 10: Without using a calculator, find $\sqrt{6^2 + 8^2}$

Solution: A square root symbol is treated like parentheses. You do the inside calculation first:

$$\sqrt{6^2 + 8^2} = \sqrt{36 + 64} = \sqrt{100} = 10$$

The TABE has only multiple-choice questions. However, at this point, you should try all the problems without guessing.

 Let's do some exercises.

No calculator should be used for these exercises.

Exercise 1: The whole numbers between 7 and 11 inclusive are

A. 7, 9, 11   D. 7, 8, 9, 10, 11

B. 8, 9, 10   E. None of these

C. 7, 11

Exercise 2: The prime numbers between 40 and 50 are

A. 41, 42, 43, 44, 45, 46, 47, 48, 49

B. 41, 43, 45, 47, 49

C. 41, 43, 47

D. 40, 41, 42, 43, 44, 45, 46, 47, 48, 49, 50

E. None of these

Exercise 3: Multiples of 7 between 60 and 80 are

A. 67, 77   D. 62, 67, 71, 73, 79

B. 63, 70, 77   E. None of these

C. 65, 70, 75

Exercise 4:   80 as the product of primes is

A. 40(2)   D. (2)(2)(2)(2)5

B. 10(4)(2)   E. None of these

C. 2(2)(2)10

Exercise 5:   All factors of 18 are

A. 2, 3, 6, 9   D. 1, 2, 3, 6, 9, 18

B. 1, 2, 3, 6, 9   E. None of these

C. 2, 3

Exercise 6: $3^7 \times 3^3 =$

A. 3^{10} D. 9^7

B. 3^{21} E. None of these

C. 3^{-4}

Exercise 7: $\dfrac{6^7}{6^4} =$

A. 6^{11} D. 1^{11}

B. 6^{28} E. None of these

C. 6^3

Exercise 8: $4^3 3^3 4^8 3^7 =$

A. 12^{24} D. $4^{24} 3^{21}$

B. 12^{504} E. None of these

C. $4^{11} 3^{10}$

Exercise 9: $10^{10} 10^9 10 =$

A. 10^{20} D. 1000^{900}

B. 10^{19} E. None of these

C. 1000^{19}

Exercise 10: $\dfrac{7^9 9^7}{7^3 9^{21}} =$

    A. $\dfrac{7^3}{9^3}$ D. $\dfrac{7^{27}}{9^{147}}$

    B. $7^3 9^3$ E. None of these

    C. $\dfrac{7^6}{9^{14}}$

Exercise 11: $100 - (5)(2) =$

    A. 190   D. 40

    B. 93   E. None of these

    C. 90

Exercise 12: $80 \div 4 \times 2 =$

    A. 160   D. 10

    B. 80   E. None of these

    C. 40

Exercise 13: $80 \times 4 \div 2 =$

    A. 160   D. 10

    B. 80   E. None of these

    C. 40

Exercise 14: $\sqrt{100 - 2(32)} =$

    A. 9   D. 6

    B. 8   E. None of these

    C. 7

Exercise 15: $2^2 + 2^3 + 2^4 =$

    A. 2^5 D. $2^5 - 8$

    B. $2^5 - 1$ E. None of these

    C. $2^5 - 2$

Exercise 16: $(10 - 2)(10 + 2) - 4^3 =$

    A. 1   **D.** 2^5

    B. 2^3 **E.** None of these

    C. 2^4

Exercise 17: $\dfrac{(3^3 - 3^2)}{3^2} =$

    A. 1   **D.** 4

    B. 2   **E.** None of these

    C. 3

Exercise 18: $(3 - 2)^{111} =$

    A. 0   **D.** $3^{111} - 2^{111}$

    B. 1   **E.** None of these

    C. 111

Exercise 19: $\sqrt{9 + 16} =$

    A. 3   **D.** 7

    B. 4   **E.** None of these

    C. 5

Exercise 20: $\dfrac{2^4 + 4^2}{40 - (2)4} =$

    A. 0   **D.** Some number greater than 2

    B. 1   **E.** None of these

    C. 2

 Let's look at the answers

Answer 1:   D: *Inclusive* means including the two end numbers

Answer 2:   C

Answer 3:   B

Answer 4:   D

Answer 5:   D

Answer 6:   A: Add the exponents; the base stays the same

Answer 7:   C: Subtract the exponents; the base stays the same

Answer 8:   C: When the bases are the same, add the exponents, leaving the bases the same

Answer 9:   A: $10 = 10^1$; add the exponents; the base stays the same

Answer 10:   C: Subtract the exponents; the base stays the same; the answer goes where the exponent with the larger exponent was located.

Answer 11:   C: $100 - 10$

Answer 12:   C: Do the multiplication and division operations in the order presented: $20(2) = 40$

Answer 13:   A: Again, do the multiplication and division operations in the order presented: $\dfrac{320}{2} = 160$

Answer 14:   D: $\sqrt{100 - 64} = \sqrt{36} = 6$

Answer 15:   E: $4 + 8 + 16 = 28$

Answer 16:   D: $96 - 64 = 32 = 2^5$

Answer 17:   B: $\dfrac{(27 - 9)}{9} = \dfrac{18}{9} = 2$

Answer 18:   B: 1 to any power is 1

Answer 19:   C: Add first; the square root of 25 is 5

Answer 20:   B: $\dfrac{(16 + 16)}{(40 - 8)} = \dfrac{32}{32} = 1$

CHAPTER 2: *Integers and Their Notation*

" *Knowing your plusses and minuses will help you succeed.* "

INTEGERS

The integers are 0, ±1, ±2, ±3, ±4, . . . , where ±4 means both +4 and −4.

We could also write the integers like this: . . . −3, −2, −1, 0, 1, 2, 3, . . .

Notes

1. We read −3 as "minus 3," but 7 and +7 are the same, so we don't always say "plus."
2. Remember that the three dots at the ends mean the numbers go on forever in either direction.

We know that −3 > −5, because −3 is to the right of −5 on the number line.

Similarly, −4 < 2, because any negative is to the left of any positive.

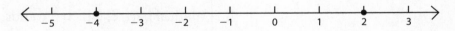

Now, let's add, multiply, divide, and subtract integers.

Adding and Subtracting Integers

Rule 1: If all the signs are the *same*, add the numbers (add the numerical parts), ignoring the sign, and use that sign in your answer.

Rule 2: If the signs are different, sum all the positives and all the negatives separately, as in Rule 1, and then subtract the two numerals and put the sign of the larger numeral in your answer.

There are only two true subtraction problems:

A. $7 - (+3)$, a number, followed by a minus sign, followed by a signed number in parenthesis.
$7 - (+3) = 7 + (-3) = 4$
The reason? Minus a plus is the same as plus a minus.

B. $7 - (-8) = 7 + (+8) = 15$ because minus a minus is the same as a plus.

Example 1: Evaluate the following:

Problems	Solutions
a. $6 + 7 + 3$	16 (or + 16)
b. $-7 - 2 - 9$	-18

Example 2:

Problems	Solutions
a: $7 - 9$	-2: The signs are different, $+7$ and -9. Subtract the numerical parts, $9 - 7 = 2$; use the sign of the larger numerical part, 9, which is minus.
b. $6 - 2$	4: The signs are different; $6 - 2 = 4$; the larger, 6, has a $+$ sign, so the answer is 4 (or $+4$).
c. $-6 + 2 + 3$	-1: The signs are different. The negative number is 6, and the sum of the positive numbers is 5. Subtract the numerical parts, $6 - 5 = 1$; use the sign of the larger numerical part, 6, which is minus.
d. $-5 + 12 + 1 - 4$	4, or $+4$: This is similar to part c; we get $13 - 9 = 4$; because 13 is positive, the answer is positive.

Multiplying and Dividing Integers

There are two basic rules for multiplying (or dividing) numbers with unlike signs:

Rule 1: A positive times a negative is a negative; a positive divided by a negative is a negative.

Rule 2: A negative times a negative is a positive; a negative divided by a negative is a positive.

Another way to state the above rules is:

Rule 3: If you are multiplying or dividing like signs, the answer is always *positive*, and if you are multiplying or dividing unlike signs, the answer is always *negative*.

The following two rules work if the problem has only multiplications and divisions.

Rule 4: If there is an odd number of minus signs, the answer is *negative*.

Rule 5: If there is an even number of minus signs, the answer is *positive*.

Example 3:   Find $\dfrac{(-4)(-6)(+2)}{(-1)(-2)(-3)}$

Solution: $\dfrac{48}{-6} = -8$ Note also that because there are 5 (an odd number of) minus signs, the answer is negative.

Example 4:

Problems	Solutions
a. $6 - 4 * 5$	$6 - 20 = -14$
b. $(6 - 4) * 5$	$2(5) = 10$
c. $(6 - 4)5$	$2(5) = 10$. Note that this is the same as b.
d. $3^3 - 4^3 - 11$	$27 - 64 - 11 = -48$
e. $\dfrac{1^{100} - 3^4}{4 - 12 \times 2}$	$\dfrac{1 - 81}{4 - 24} = \dfrac{-80}{-20} = 4$
f. $-\sqrt{6^2 - 4^2} - 11$	$-\sqrt{36 - 16} - 11 = -\sqrt{9} = -3$
g. $-8 - (+2) - (-3)$	$-8 + (-2) + 3$, or $-8 - 2 + 3 = -7$
h. $4 - (+3) - (-3)$	$4 - 3 + 3 = 4$

You may see another notation for negative numbers on the TABE, so I will include it here. Instead of writing -6 for minus 6, sometimes the TABE writes $^-6$.

Example 5:

Problems	Solutions
a. $^-4 + {}^-3$	Think $(-4) + (-3) = -7$, or $^-7$.
b. $^-8 - {}^+5$	Think $(-8) - (+5) = (-8) + (-5) = -13$, or $^-13$.

c. $^-7 - {}^-9$ Think $(-7) - (-9) = (-7) + (+9) = 2$, or $+2$, or $^+2$

d. $(^-8)(^-4)$ Think $(-8) \times (-4) = 32$, or $+32$, or $^+32$

e. $\dfrac{^-10}{^+2}$ Think $(-10) \div (+2) = -5$, or $^-5$

MORE LAWS OF EXPONENTS

We must learn a little bit more about exponents.

What if the exponent is 0? We know that if we have $\dfrac{4^6}{4^6}$, the answer is 1 because anything (other than 0) divided by itself is 1. However, if we follow the division rule to subtract exponents, $\dfrac{4^6}{4^6} = 4^{6-6} = 4^0 = 4^{6-6} = 4^0$. This leads us to the fact that

$$n^0 = 1 \text{ if } n \text{ is not zero.}$$

For example, $(3\text{pigs})^0 = 1$, whereas $3(\text{pigs})^0 = 3(1) = 3$.

But what if the exponent is a negative number? **Negative exponents** mean reciprocals; they have nothing to do with negative numbers! A **reciprocal** is found by simply flipping the number over the fraction bar. If you multiply a number by its reciprocal, you always get 1. For example, the reciprocal of a is $\dfrac{1}{a}$, and $a \times \dfrac{1}{a} = 1$.

So $b^{-k} = \dfrac{1}{b^k}$ and $\dfrac{1}{7^{-2}} = 7^2$.

Now that we know about negative exponents, let's revisit division of exponential numbers.

Example 6: $\dfrac{3^4}{3^9}$

Solution: Following the rule for division, subtracting the exponents gives $3^{(4-9)} = 3^{-5}$. Looking at the solution in another way, if we write out the problem, $\dfrac{3^4}{3^9} = \dfrac{3 \times 3 \times 3 \times 3}{3 \times 3 \times 3 \times 3 \times 3 \times 3 \times 3 \times 3 \times 3}$. We see four of the 3's cancel from the top and bottom (remembering that $\dfrac{3}{3} = 1$), so $\dfrac{3^4}{3^9} = \dfrac{1}{3^5}$, and the answer is $3^{-5} = \dfrac{1}{3^5}$.

Example 7:

Problems	Solutions
a. 5^{-2}	$\dfrac{1}{5^2} = \dfrac{1}{25}$
b. $1/6^{-3}$	$6^3 = 216$
c. $(-5)^{-4}$	$\dfrac{1}{(-5)^4} = \dfrac{1}{(-5)(-5)(-5)(-5)} = \dfrac{1}{625}$ (even number of minus signs)
d. $(-2)^{-3}$	$\dfrac{1}{(-2)^3} = \dfrac{1}{(-2)(-2)(-2)} = -\dfrac{1}{8}$ (odd number of minus signs)
e. 10^{-8}	$\dfrac{1}{10^8} = \dfrac{1}{100,000,000}$ (one divided by one hundred million)
f. $\dfrac{1}{10^{-4}}$	$10^4 = 10,000$ (ten thousand)

Negative exponents are used a lot in scientific notation, which is discussed next.

SCIENTIFIC NOTATION

An example of **scientific notation** is the number 3.27×10^{14} or 4.32×10^{-10}. The numerical part (here, 3.27 or 4.32) always has only one digit to the left of the decimal point, and the exponent of 10 tells the size of the number.

To write a number in scientific notation, place the decimal point after the first nonzero integer. Count the places you would have to move the decimal from its original position, left or right, to determine the exponent of 10. If you move the decimal to the left, your original number was very large, and the exponent of 10 is positive. If you move the decimal to the right, your original number was very small, and the exponent of 10 is negative. Examples 8 and 9 show how this works.

Example 8: In chemistry, there is a quantity called Avogadro's number, which is 602,300,000,000,000,000,000,000 molecules per mole. This is very impractical to write, or even to say (six hundred two sextillion, three hundred quintillion). How would you write this in scientific notation?

Solution: Written in scientific notation, the number is simply 6.023×10^{23}. The decimal is moved from the end of the very large number 23 places to the left, so only one integer is before it.

Note *On your calculator, the number would be 6.023   23. Only the exponent is shown, not the base, which is 10.*

Example 9:   Write the width of the hydrogen atom in meters in scientific notation. Oh, the number is very, very small—it is .000 000 000 000 000 000 000 000 000 91 meters. It is impractical to write it as

$$\frac{91}{10,000,000,000,000,000,000,000,000,000,000}, \text{ or to read it as ninety one}$$

dectillionths.

Solution: We move the decimal 31 places to the right, so it appears right after the first nonzero integer, 9. The number, in scientific notation thus becomes 9.1×10^{-31} meters.

Note *Remember that the negative exponent here means it is on the bottom of the fraction. On the calculator it would be 9.1   −31.*

Example 10:   Write in scientific notation:

Problems	Solutions
a. 97802	9.7802×10^4
b. .003	3×10^{-3}
c. 1,000,000	1×10^6
d. .723	7.23×10^{-1}
e. 63	6.3×10^1
f. 206,000,000	2.06×10^8

One other term that comes up occasionally when comparing numbers is **order of magnitude**, which refers to a factor of 10. In comparing 300 and 3000, for example, $300 = 3 \times 10^2$ and $3,000 = 3 \times 10^3$. Thus, 3,000 is one order of magnitude larger than 300 because the exponents of 10 differ by 1.

EXPANDED NOTATION

We can write whole numbers, decimals, and combinations in powers of 10. This is called **expanded notation**.

We have seen in scientific notation that numbers can be written using powers of 10. Let's do a little more.

Ten =	$10 = 10^1$
One hundred =	$100 = 10^2$
One thousand =	$1{,}000 = 10^3$
Ten thousand =	$10{,}000 = 10^4$
One hundred thousand =	$100{,}000 = 10^5$
One million =	$1{,}000{,}000 = 10^6$

We can write decimals the same way:

One tenth =	$.1 = 10^{-1}$
One hundredth =	$.01 = 10^{-2}$
One thousandth =	$.001 = 10^{-3}$

So, to write 3,456 in expanded notation, we separate each numeral into its value, as follows:

$$3{,}456 = 3000 + 400 + 50 + 6 = 3 \times 10^3 + 4 \times 10^2 + 5 \times 10^1 + 6$$

If any of the digits are zeros, that place doesn't have a value in expanded notation. Thus,

$$5{,}000{,}800 = 5{,}000{,}000 + 800 = 5 \times 10^6 + 8 \times 10^2$$

Decimals are treated the same way. The exponents of 10 are negative numbers.

$$6.06 = 6 + .06 = 6 + 6 \times 10^{-2}$$

Example 11: Write in expanded notation:

Problems	Solutions
a. 30,460	$3 \times 10^4 + 4 \times 10^2 + 6 \times 10^1$
b. .123	$1 \times 10^{-1} + 2 \times 10^{-2} + 3 \times 10^{-3}$
c. 43.43	$4 \times 10^1 + 3 + 4 \times 10^{-1} + 3 \times 10^{-2}$
d. 123,456.789	$1 \times 10^5 + 2 \times 10^4 + 3 \times 10^3 + 4 \times 10^2 +$
	$5 \times 10^1 + 6 + 7 \times 10^{-1} + 8 \times 10^{-2} +$
	9×10^{-3}

The last problem might help to convince you that longer is not always harder. In fact, in a good precalculus course, the shorter the problem, the harder it is because the shorter ones involve more thinking.

Q Let's do some exercises.

No calculator should be used for these exercises.

Exercise 1: $4 - 7 - 3 =$

A. 9   D. -6

B. 6   E. None of these

C. 0

Exercise 2: $(-1)^{10} + (-1^{10}) =$

A. -20 D. 2

B. -2 E. None of these

C. 0

Exercise 3: $4 - 2(3) - 4(-3) =$

A. 18   D. -14

B. 10   E. None of these

C. -1

Exercise 4: $2^5 - 6^2 =$

A. 2   D. -4

B. 0   E. None of these

C. -2

Exercise 5: $3^{-4} =$

A. 12   D. $-\dfrac{1}{12}$

B. -12 E. None of these

C. $\dfrac{1}{12}$

Exercise 6: $\dfrac{1}{10^{-3}} =$

    A. -1000

    B. -30

    C. 30

    D. 1000

    E. None of these

Exercise 7: $\dfrac{8^{-2}}{5^{-1}} =$

    A. 80

    B. $\dfrac{64}{5}$

    C. $-\dfrac{64}{5}$

    D. $-\dfrac{5}{64}$

    E. None of these

Exercise 8: $\dfrac{0}{4} - 0(4) - 4 =$

    A. 0

    B. -4

    C. -8

    D. -16

    E. None of these

Exercise 9: $(5 \times 3)^0 + 5 \times 3^0 =$

    A. 20

    B. 16

    C. 15

    D. 6

    E. None of these

Exercise 10:   7300 in scientific notation is

    A. 73×10^2

    B. 7.3×10^2

    C. 73×10^3

    D. 7.3×10^3

    E. None of these

Exercise 11: $.0035 \times 20 \times 10^{-4} =$

A. .0007

B. .00007

C. .000007

D. .0000007

E. None of these

Exercise 12: $10^{-5} \times 10^{-5} =$

A. 10^{25}

B. 10^{10}

C. 1

D. 10^{-10}

E. None of these

Exercise 13: $^-7 + {}^-2 + {}^+6 =$

A. 84

B. 20

C. -1

D. -3

E. None of these

Exercise 14: $(-2)(-3)(-1)(1)(-2)(-10) =$

A. -120

B. -19

C. -1

D. 0

E. None of these

Exercise 15: In expanded notation, 3,407 is

A. $3 \times 10^2 + 4 \times 10 + 7$

B. $3 \times 10^3 + 4 \times 10^2 + 7 \times 10$

C. $3 \times 10^3 + 4 \times 10^2 + 7$

D. 84×10^{12}

E. None of these

Exercise 16: $5^0 + 5^1 + 5^2 + 5^3 =$

A. 5^4

B. $5^4 - 5$

C. 160

D. 156

E. None of these

Exercise 17: $(^-3 \times {}^-5) + (-3)(-5) =$

  A. -30 **D.** 100

  B. 0 **E.** None of these

  C. 30

Exercise 18: $-3 - 4(-5) - 6 =$

  A. -18 **D.** 11

  B. -13 **E.** None of these

  C. 1

Exercise 19: $(-5 - 5)(-5 + 4) =$

  A. -10 **D.** 1

  B. -1 **E.** None of these

  C. 0

Exercise 20: $(-1)^3 - (-1)^4 + (-1)^5 - (-1)^6 =$

  A. -4 **D.** 2

  B. -2 **E.** None of these

  C. 0

 **Let's look at the answers**

Answer 1:   D: $-3 + -3 = -6$

Answer 2:   C: $1 - 1 = 0$

Answer 3:   B: $4 - 6 + 12 = 10$

Answer 4:   D: $32 - 36$

Answer 5:   E: $\dfrac{1}{3^4} = \dfrac{1}{81}$

Answer 6:   D: $\dfrac{1}{10^{-3}} = \dfrac{1}{\frac{1}{10^3}} = 10^3 = 1000$

Answer 7:   E: Negative exponents have nothing to do with negative numbers

$\dfrac{8^{-2}}{5^{-1}} = \dfrac{5^1}{8^2} = \dfrac{5}{64}$

Answer 8:   B: $0 - 0 - 4 = -4$

Answer 9:   D: $1 + 5(1) = 1 + 5 = 6$

Answer 10:   D

Answer 11:   C

Answer 12:   D: Exponents are added

Answer 13:   D: $-9 + 6$

Answer 14:   A

Answer 15:   C

Answer 16:   D: $1 + 5 + 25 + 125 = 156$

Answer 17:   C: $15 + 15$

Answer 18:   D: $-3 + 20 - 6 = 20 - 9 = 11$

Answer 19:   E: $(-10)(-1) = 10$

Answer 20:   A: $-1 - 1 - 1 - 1 = -4$

Let's go on.

CHAPTER 3: *Decimals and Fractions and More*

"*One must master the parts as well as the whole to fully understand.* "

Here we review decimals, fractions, and percentages, with which some of you are already familiar, and we'll throw in a bit about rounding and about absolute value. Because the TABE does not allow calculators for part of the exam, you might want to practice these skills with just pencil and paper, so we've included lots of practice problems.

DECIMALS

Rule 1: When adding or subtracting, line up the decimal points.

Example 1: Add: 3.1416 + 234.72 + 86

Solution:

$$
\begin{array}{r}
3.1416 \\
234.72 \\
+ \ 86. \\
\hline
323.8616
\end{array}
$$

Example 2: Subtract: 56.7 − 8.82

Solution:

$$
\begin{array}{r}
56.70 \\
- \ 8.82 \\
\hline
47.88
\end{array}
$$

Rule 2: In multiplying numbers, count the number of decimal places and add them. In the product, this will be the number of decimal places for the decimal.

Example 3:   Multiply: $45.67 \times .987$

Solution:

$$
\begin{array}{rl}
45.67 & \text{(2 places)} \\
\times \quad .987 & \text{(3 places)} \\
\hline
45.07629 & \text{(5 places)}
\end{array}
$$

If you're curious, the reason it's five places is that if you multiply hundredths by thousandths, you get hundred-thousandths, which is five places. Fortunately, the TABE does not ask you to do pure long multiplications like this.

Rule 3: When you divide, move the decimal point in the divisor and the dividend the same number of places.

$$\overset{\text{Quotient}}{\text{Divisor}\overline{)\text{Dividend}}}$$

Example 4: $.004\overline{)23.1}$

Solution: $4\overline{)23100}$ with quotient 5775

Why is this true? If we write the division as a fraction, it would be $\frac{23.1}{.004}$. Multiplying the numerator and denominator by 1000, we get $\frac{23.1}{.004} = \frac{23.1 \times 1000}{.004 \times 1000} = \frac{23100}{4}$. When you multiply by 1, the fraction doesn't change. Because $\frac{1000}{1000} = 1$, the fraction is the same.

Rule 4: When reading a number with a decimal, read the whole part, only say the word *and* when you reach the decimal point, then read the part after the decimal point as if it were a whole number, and say the last decimal place. Whew!

Example 5:   State each number in words.

Problems	Solutions
4.3	Four and three tenths
2,006.73	Two-thousand six and seventy-three hundredths
1,000,017.009	One million seventeen and nine thousandths

Now, let's go over fractions.

FRACTIONS

The top of a fraction is called the **numerator**; the bottom is the **denominator**.

Rule 1: If the bottoms of two fractions are the same, the bigger the top, the bigger the fraction.

Example 6:   Suppose I am a smart first grader. Can you explain to me which is bigger, $\frac{3}{5}$ or $\frac{4}{5}$?

Solution: Suppose we have a pizza pie. Then $\frac{3}{5}$ means we divide a pie into 5 equal parts, and I get 3. And $\frac{4}{5}$ means I get 4 pieces out of 5. So $\frac{3}{5} < \frac{4}{5}$.

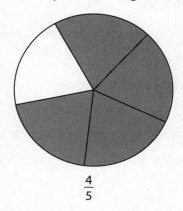
$$\frac{4}{5}$$

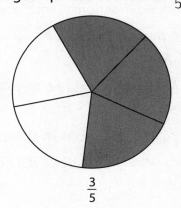
$$\frac{3}{5}$$

Rule 2: If the tops of two fractions are the same, the bigger the bottom, the smaller the fraction.

Example 7:   Which fraction, $\frac{3}{5}$ or $\frac{3}{4}$, is bigger?

Solution: Use another pizza pie example. In comparing $\frac{3}{5}$ and $\frac{3}{4}$, we get the same number of pieces (3). However, if the pie is divided into 4, the pieces are bigger, so $\frac{3}{5} < \frac{3}{4}$.

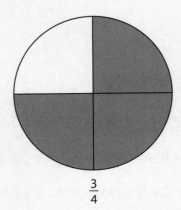

$$\frac{3}{4}$$

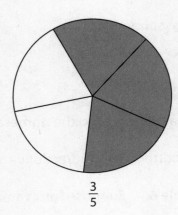

$$\frac{3}{5}$$

Rule 3: If the tops and bottoms are different, find the least common denominator (LCD) and compare the tops.

Before we get into this section, the teacher in me must tell you we really are talking about rational numbers, not fractions. There are two definitions.

Definition 1: A **rational** number is any integer divided by an integer, with the denominator not equaling zero.

Definition 2: A **rational** number is any repeating or terminating decimal.

Note *Technically, $\frac{\pi}{6}$ is a fraction but not a rational number. We will use the term* fraction *here instead of rational number. If it is negative, we will say, "Negative fraction." Note the following facts about fractions:*

- $3 < 4$, but $-3 > -4$. Similarly, $\frac{3}{5} < \frac{4}{5}$, but $-\frac{3}{5} > -\frac{4}{5}$. We will do more of this later.
- A fraction is bigger than one if the numerator is bigger than the denominator.
- A fraction is less than one if the numerator is less than the denominator.
- A fraction is less than $\frac{1}{2}$ if the bottom is more than twice the top
- To double a fraction, either double the top or half the bottom.
- Adding the same number top and bottom to a fraction makes it closer to 1.

Reducing Fractions

When working with fractions, we would like to reduce, or simplify, fractions as much as possible because that simplifies the work we have to do later.

Example 8:   Reduce the fraction $\frac{4}{6}$.

Solution: To reduce a fraction, we must find a number that is a divisor of (meaning it divides evenly into) both the numerator and denominator. We see that 2 divides evenly into both 4 and 6. 2 into 4 is 2, and 2 into 6 is 3. So $\frac{4}{6}$ reduces to $\frac{2}{3}$. We write $\frac{4}{6} = \frac{2}{3}$. Another way to look at reducing fractions is to break down the fraction into primes, so we can write $\frac{4}{6} = \frac{2 \times 2}{2 \times 3}$. A 2 in the top cancels with a 2 in the bottom because any number other than zero divided by itself is 1. Again, the fraction reduces to $\frac{2}{3}$.

 Notes

1. You should pick whichever method works best for you.

2. You might use both methods, depending on the problem.

3. The number you use to reduce the fraction doesn't even have to be a prime. The same number just has to be a factor in the top and bottom of the fraction.

Example 9:   Reduce the following fractions:

<u>Problems</u>	<u>Solutions</u>
a. $\frac{8}{10}$	$\frac{4}{5}$
b. $\frac{10}{25}$	$\frac{2}{5}$
c. $\frac{8}{14}$	$\frac{4}{7}$
d. $\frac{8}{12}$	$\frac{2}{3}$
e. $\frac{30}{45}$	$\frac{2}{3}$
f. $\frac{36}{48}$	$\frac{3}{4}$
g. $\frac{24}{49}$	Some fractions can't be reduced

Mixed Numbers and Improper Fractions

A **mixed number** is a whole number plus a fraction. An **improper fraction** is a fraction for which the numerator is bigger than or equal to the denominator.

To change a mixed number to an improper fraction, change the whole number to a fraction with the same denominator as the fraction part of the mixed number. Do this by multiplying the whole number, top and bottom (remember, a whole number has a denominator of 1) by the denominator of the fraction part.

Example 10: Change $2\frac{1}{3}$ to an improper fraction.

Solution: We multiply 2 by $\frac{3}{3}$ to get $\frac{6}{3}$ and add that to $\frac{1}{3}$ to get the answer: $\frac{7}{3}$. Let's see why.

If we write 2 as thirds, we get 6 thirds, as you see in the picture below. One third more makes $\frac{7}{3}$.

A faster way to do this computation is just to multiply the whole number by the denominator in the mixed number, and add the numerator of the fraction to get the new numerator. The denominator stays the same. For Example 10, $2(3) + 1 = 7$, so the answer is $\frac{7}{3}$.

To change an improper fraction to a mixed number, reverse the above procedure. Divide the denominator into the numerator to get the whole number part of the mixed number. The fraction part is the remainder over the denominator.

Example 11: Change $\frac{38}{5}$ to a mixed number.

Solution: If we divide 5 into 38; we get 7 with a remainder of 3, which we write as $7\frac{3}{5}$.

Let's try some more examples.

Example 12: Change to a mixed number:

Problems	Solutions
a. $\frac{9}{2}$	$4\frac{1}{2}$
b. $\frac{16}{3}$	$5\frac{1}{3}$
c. $\frac{18}{4}$	$4\frac{2}{4}$, or $4\frac{1}{2}$
d. $\frac{27}{5}$	$5\frac{2}{5}$

e. $\dfrac{41}{6}$ $\qquad\qquad$ $6\dfrac{5}{6}$

f. $\dfrac{62}{7}$ $\qquad\qquad$ $8\dfrac{6}{7}$

g. $\dfrac{22}{8}$ $\qquad\qquad$ $2\dfrac{6}{8}$ or $2\dfrac{3}{4}$

h. $\dfrac{83}{9}$ $\qquad\qquad$ $9\dfrac{2}{9}$

i. $\dfrac{73}{10}$ $\qquad\qquad$ $7\dfrac{3}{10}$

Adding and Subtracting Fractions

If the denominators are the same, add or subtract the tops, keep the bottom the same, and reduce if necessary.

$$\frac{7}{43} + \frac{11}{43} - \frac{2}{43} = \frac{16}{43}$$

$$\frac{2}{9} + \frac{4}{9} = \frac{6}{9} = \frac{2}{3}$$

$$\frac{a}{m} + \frac{b}{m} - \frac{c}{m} = \frac{a+b-c}{m}$$

There is much more to talk about if the denominators are unlike.

The quickest way to add (or subtract) fractions with different denominators, especially if they contain letters or if the denominators are small, is to multiply each fraction by the LCD. The LCD is really just the least common multiple, LCM. This consists of three words: **multiple**, **common**, and **least**.

Example 13: What is the LCM of 6 and 8?

Solution:

Multiples of 6 are 6, 12, 18, 24, 30, 36, 42, 48, 54, 60, 66, 72, 78,…
Multiples of 8 are 8, 16, 24, 32, 40, 48, 56, 64, 72, 80,…
Common multiples of 6 and 8 are 24, 48, 72, 96, 120,…
The **LEAST common multiple** of 6 and 8 is 24.

When adding or subtracting fractions, multiply the top and bottom of each fraction by the LCM divided by the denominator:

$$\frac{a}{b} - \frac{x}{y} = \left(\frac{a}{b} \times \frac{y}{y}\right) - \left(\frac{x}{y} \times \frac{b}{b}\right) = \frac{ay}{by} - \frac{bx}{by} = \frac{ay - bx}{by}$$

$$\frac{7}{20} - \frac{3}{11} = \left(\frac{7}{20} \times \frac{11}{11}\right) - \left(\frac{3}{11} \times \frac{20}{20}\right) = \frac{7(11) - 3(20)}{20(11)} = \frac{17}{220}$$

Example 14:   Add $\frac{5}{6} + \frac{3}{8} + \frac{2}{9}$

Solution: To find the LCD, take multiples of the largest denominator, 9, and see which one is also a multiple of the others (6 and 8): 9, 18, 27, 36, 45, 54, 63, 72. The LCD is 72, so we have:

$$\frac{5}{6} = \frac{5}{6} \times \frac{12}{12} = \frac{60}{72}$$

$$\frac{3}{8} = \frac{3}{8} \times \frac{9}{9} = \frac{27}{72}$$

$$\frac{2}{9} = \frac{2}{9} \times \frac{8}{8} = \frac{16}{72}$$

Adding these, we get $\frac{103}{72}$, or $1\frac{31}{72}$. You may have to add fractions like this on the TABE.

Example 15:   Add: $2\frac{3}{4} + 5\frac{1}{6}$

Solution: The LCD (the LCM for 4 and 6) is 12, so we multiply the top and bottom of each fraction by 12 divided by the denominator. For the first fraction, because $\frac{12}{4} = 3$, we multiply by $\frac{3}{3}$. (Remember, this is equal to 1, so the value of the fraction doesn't change.) For the second fraction, because $\frac{12}{6} = 2$, we multiply by $\frac{2}{2}$. So we get $2\frac{3}{4} = 2\frac{3 \times 3}{4 \times 3} = 2\frac{9}{12}$, which we will add to $5\frac{1}{6} = 5\frac{1 \times 2}{6 \times 2} = 5\frac{2}{12}$. The answer is $2\frac{9}{12} + 5\frac{2}{12} = 7\frac{11}{12}$.

Example 16:   Add: $5\frac{2}{3} + 4\frac{8}{9}$.

Solution: The LCD is 9, so $5\frac{2}{3} = 5\frac{2 \times 3}{3 \times 3} = 5\frac{6}{9}$, and $4\frac{8}{9}$ doesn't have to be changed. Adding, we get $5\frac{6}{9} + 4\frac{8}{9} = 9\frac{14}{9}$. But $\frac{14}{9}$ is an improper fraction equal to $1\frac{5}{9}$. So the answer is $9 + 1\frac{5}{9} = 10\frac{5}{9}$.

Example 17: Subtract: $7\frac{5}{8} - 2\frac{1}{2}$

Solution: The LCD is 8. $7\frac{5}{8}$ is okay, and $2\frac{1}{2} = 2\frac{1\times4}{2\times4} = 2\frac{4}{8}$. Subtracting the whole

parts, we get $7 - 2 = 5$, and subtracting the fractional parts, we get

$\frac{5}{8} - \frac{4}{8} = \frac{1}{8}$, so the answer is $5\frac{1}{8}$.

Example 18: Subtract: $8\frac{1}{3} - 2\frac{4}{5}$.

Solution: The LCD is 15. So $8\frac{1}{3} = 8\frac{1\times5}{3\times5} = 8\frac{5}{15}$ and $2\frac{4}{5} = 2\frac{4\times3}{5\times3} = 2\frac{12}{15}$. Subtract-

ing, we see that $\frac{12}{15}$ is larger than $\frac{5}{15}$. So we need to borrow $1 = \frac{15}{15}$ from

the 8, and we get $8\frac{5}{15} = 7 + 1 + \frac{5}{15} = 7 + \frac{15}{15} + \frac{5}{15} = 7\frac{20}{15}$. So the prob-

lem becomes $7\frac{20}{15} - 2\frac{12}{15} = 5\frac{8}{15}$.

Notes

1. Some of these steps you can do in your head. They were all written out here for ease in understanding.

2. Occasionally the last fraction has to be reduced. So reduce it if necessary.

Multiplication of Fractions

To multiply fractions, multiply the numerators and multiply the denominators, reducing as you go. With multiplication, it is *not* necessary to have the same denominators.

$$\frac{3}{7} \times \frac{4}{11} = \frac{12}{77}$$

$$\frac{a}{b} \times \frac{c}{d} = \frac{a\times c}{b\times d}$$

$$\frac{50}{15} \times \frac{27}{8} = \frac{25}{15} \times \frac{27}{4} = \frac{25}{5} \times \frac{9}{4} = \frac{5}{1} \times \frac{9}{4} = \frac{45}{4}, \text{ or } 11\frac{1}{4}$$

$$3\frac{3}{4} \times 1\frac{1}{5} = \frac{15}{4} \times \frac{6}{5} = \frac{15}{2} \times \frac{3}{5} = \frac{3}{2} \times \frac{3}{1} = \frac{9}{2}, \text{ or } 4\frac{1}{2}.$$

To **invert** a fraction means to turn it upside down. The new fraction is called the **reciprocal** of the original fraction.

The reciprocal of $\frac{2}{3}$ is $\frac{3}{2}$; the reciprocal of -5 is $\frac{-1}{5}$; the reciprocal of a is $\frac{1}{a}$ if $a \neq 0$.

Division of Fractions

To divide fractions, invert the second fraction and multiply, reducing if necessary. For example,

$$\frac{3}{4} \div \frac{11}{5} = \frac{3}{4} \times \frac{5}{11} = \frac{15}{44}$$

$$\frac{m}{n} \div \frac{p}{q} = \frac{m}{n} \times \frac{q}{p} = \frac{m \times q}{n \times p}$$

$$\frac{1}{4} \div 5 = \frac{1}{4} \times \frac{1}{5} = \frac{1}{20}$$

$$4\frac{3}{5} \div 1\frac{1}{10} = \frac{23}{5} \div \frac{11}{10} = \frac{23}{5} \times \frac{10}{11} = \frac{23}{1} \times \frac{2}{11} = \frac{46}{11}, \text{ or } 4\frac{2}{11}$$

Example 19: <u>Problems</u>   <u>Solutions</u>

a. $\dfrac{7}{9} - \dfrac{3}{22} =$ $\dfrac{127}{198}$

b. $\dfrac{3}{4} + \dfrac{5}{6} - \dfrac{1}{8} =$ $\dfrac{35}{24}, \text{ or } 1\dfrac{11}{24}$

c. $\dfrac{3}{10} + \dfrac{2}{15} - \dfrac{4}{5} =$ $\dfrac{-11}{30}$

d. $\dfrac{1}{4} + \dfrac{1}{8} + \dfrac{7}{16} =$ $\dfrac{13}{16}$

e. $2 + \dfrac{2}{3} + \dfrac{2}{9} + \dfrac{2}{27} =$ $2\dfrac{26}{27}, \text{ or } \dfrac{80}{27}$

f. $\dfrac{5}{24} - \dfrac{7}{18} =$ $-\dfrac{13}{72}$

g. $\dfrac{10}{99} - \dfrac{9}{100} =$ $\dfrac{109}{9900}$

h. $\dfrac{5}{36} + \dfrac{5}{27} + \dfrac{7}{24} =$ $\dfrac{133}{216}$

i. $\dfrac{2}{45} + \dfrac{1}{375} + \dfrac{8}{27} =$ $\dfrac{1159}{3375}$

j. $\dfrac{3}{10,000} + \dfrac{1}{180} + \dfrac{5}{12} =$ $\dfrac{38,027}{90,000}$

k. $\dfrac{7}{9} \times \dfrac{5}{3} =$ $\dfrac{35}{27}, \text{ or } 1\dfrac{8}{27}$

l. $\dfrac{11}{12} \div \dfrac{9}{11} =$　　　　　　$\dfrac{121}{108}$, or $1\dfrac{13}{108}$

m. $\dfrac{5}{9} \times \dfrac{6}{7} =$　　　　　　$\dfrac{10}{21}$

n. $\dfrac{12}{13} \div \dfrac{8}{39} =$　　　　　　$\dfrac{9}{2}$, or $4\dfrac{1}{2}$

o. $\dfrac{4}{9} \times \dfrac{63}{122} =$　　　　　　$\dfrac{14}{61}$

p. $\dfrac{10}{12} \div \dfrac{15}{40} =$　　　　　　$\dfrac{20}{9}$, or $2\dfrac{2}{9}$

q. $\dfrac{100}{350} \times \dfrac{49}{8} =$　　　　　　$\dfrac{7}{4}$, or $1\dfrac{3}{4}$

r. $\dfrac{2}{3} \div 12 =$　　　　　　$\dfrac{1}{18}$

s. $\dfrac{2}{3} \times \dfrac{3}{4} \times \dfrac{4}{5} \times \dfrac{5}{6} \times \dfrac{6}{7} =$　　　$\dfrac{2}{7}$

t. $\dfrac{5}{8} \times \dfrac{7}{6} \div \dfrac{35}{24} =$　　　　　$\dfrac{1}{2}$

u. $4\dfrac{2}{7} + 3\dfrac{4}{7}$　　　　　　$7\dfrac{6}{7}$

v. $9\dfrac{5}{9} + 2\dfrac{5}{9}$　　　　　　$12\dfrac{1}{9}$

w. $7\dfrac{1}{5} + 4\dfrac{4}{5}$　　　　　　12

x. $4\dfrac{5}{9} + 1\dfrac{7}{9}$　　　　　　$6\dfrac{1}{3}$

y. $4\dfrac{3}{4} + 5\dfrac{1}{12}$　　　　　　$9\dfrac{5}{6}$

z. $5\dfrac{7}{8} + 9\dfrac{5}{6}$　　　　　　$14\dfrac{41}{24}$, or $15\dfrac{17}{24}$

Let's try a few with subtraction, multiplication, and division.

Example 20: <u>Problems</u>   <u>Solutions</u>

a. $7\frac{10}{11} - \frac{2}{11}$ $7\frac{8}{11}$

b. $6\frac{1}{3} - 3\frac{2}{3}$ $2\frac{2}{3}$

c. $6\frac{7}{8} - 2\frac{1}{3}$ $4\frac{13}{24}$

d. $5\frac{1}{8} - 4\frac{3}{5}$ $\frac{21}{40}$

e. $3\frac{1}{2} \times 3\frac{1}{2}$ $\frac{49}{4}$, or $12\frac{1}{4}$

f. $4\frac{1}{5} \times 1\frac{2}{7}$ $\frac{27}{5}$, or $5\frac{2}{5}$

g. $1\frac{1}{3} \div 4$ $\frac{1}{3}$

h. $3\frac{1}{5} \div 1\frac{1}{9}$ $\frac{72}{25}$, or $2\frac{22}{25}$

Changing from Decimals to Fractions and Back

To change from a decimal to a fraction, you read it and write it.

Example 21: Change 4.37 to a fraction.

Solution: You read it as 4 and 37 hundredths: $4\frac{37}{100} = \frac{437}{100}$, if necessary. That's it.

Example 22: Change to decimals:

<u>Problems</u>   <u>Solutions</u>

a. $\frac{7}{4}$ Divide 4 into 7.0000: $\div 4 = 1.75$

b. $\frac{1}{6}$ Divide 6 into 1.0000: $\div 6 = .1666\ldots = .1\overline{6}$

Notes

1. For the fractions on the TABE, the decimal will either terminate or repeat.

2. The **bar** over the six means it repeats forever; for example, $.3454545\ldots = .3\overline{45}$. means 45 repeats forever, but the 3 does not.

PERCENTAGES

% means hundredths: $1\% = \dfrac{1}{100} = .01$.

Follow these rules to change between percentages and decimals and fractions:

Rule 1: To change a percentage to a decimal, move the decimal point two places to the left and drop the % sign.

Rule 2: To change a decimal to a percentage, move the decimal point two places to the right and add a % sign.

Rule 3: To change from a percentage to a fraction, divide by 100% and simplify, or change the % sign to $\dfrac{1}{100}$ and multiply.

Rule 4: To change a fraction to a percentage, first change to a decimal, and then to a percentage.

Example 23: Change 12%, 4%, and .7% to decimals.

Solutions: $12\% = 12.\% = .12$; $4\% = 4.\% = .04$; $.7\% = .007$.

Example 24: Change .734, .2, and 34 to percentages.

Solutions: $.734 = 73.4\%$; $.2 = 20\%$; $34 = 34. = 3400\%$.

Example 25: Change 42% to a fraction.

Solution: $\dfrac{42\%}{100\%} = \dfrac{21}{50}$, or $42\% = 42 \times \dfrac{1}{100} = \dfrac{42}{100} = \dfrac{21}{50}$

Example 26: Change $\dfrac{7}{4}$ to a percentage.

Solution: $\dfrac{7}{4} = 1.75 = 175\%$

Two hundred years ago, when I was in elementary school, we had to learn the following decimal, fraction, and percentage equivalents. Because there is no calculator on this part of the test, it may be in your best interest to memorize the following. At worst, it will help you when you go shopping for anything to see if you get the correct discounts.

Fraction	Decimal	Percentage		Fraction	Decimal	Percentage
$\frac{1}{10}$	.1	10%		$\frac{5}{8}$	.625	$62\frac{1}{2}\%$
$\frac{1}{8}$	.125	$12\frac{1}{2}\%$		$\frac{2}{3}$	.6666…	$66\frac{2}{3}\%$
$\frac{1}{6}$	.1666…	$16\frac{2}{3}\%$		$\frac{7}{10}$	.7	70%
$\frac{1}{5}$	.2	20%		$\frac{3}{4}$	.75	75%
$\frac{1}{4}$	.25	25%		$\frac{8}{10}$	.8	80%
$\frac{3}{10}$	.3	30%		$\frac{5}{6}$	.8333…	$83\frac{1}{3}\%$
$\frac{1}{3}$	.3333…	$33\frac{1}{3}\%$		$\frac{7}{8}$	.875	$87\frac{1}{2}\%$
$\frac{3}{8}$	.375	$37\frac{1}{2}\%$		$\frac{9}{10}$	.9	90%
$\frac{2}{5}$	.4	40%		1	1.0	100%
$\frac{1}{2}$	.5	50%		$1\frac{1}{2}$	1.5	150%
$\frac{3}{5}$	.6	60%		2	2.0	200%

If you are good at doing percentage problems, skip this next section. Otherwise, here's a really neat way do percentage problems. Make the following pyramid:

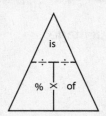

Example 27: What is 12% of 1.3?

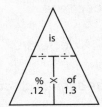

Solution:

Put .12 in the % box (always change to a decimal in this box) and 1.3 in the "of" box. It tells you to multiply .12 × 1.3 = .156. That's all there is to it.

Example 28: 8% of what is 32?

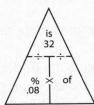

Solution:

.08 goes in the % box. 32 goes in the "is" box. 32 ÷ .08 = 400.

Example 29: 9 is what % of 8?

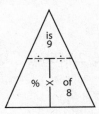

Solution:

9 goes in the "is" box. 8 goes in the "of" box. 9 ÷ 8 × 100% = 112.5%.

The goal is to be able to do percentage problems without writing the pyramid.

Example 30: In ten years, the population increases from 20,000 to 23,000. Find the actual increase and the percentage increase.

Solution: The actual increase is 23,000 − 20,000 = 3,000.

The percentage increase is $\frac{3000}{20,000} \times 100\% = 15\%$ increase.

Example 31:   The cost of producing widgets decreased from 60 cents to 50 cents. Find the actual decrease and percentage decrease.

Solution: $60 - 50 = 10$ cent decrease; $\dfrac{10}{60} = 16\dfrac{2}{3}\%$ decrease.

Note   *Percentage increases and decreases are figured on the original amount.*

Example 32:   The cost of a $2000 large-screen TV set is decreased by 30%. If there is 7% sales tax, how much do you pay?

Solution: $2000 \times .30 = \$600$ discount. $2000 - \$600 = \$1400$ cost.

$1400 \times .07$ is $98. The total price is $1400 + \$98 = \$1498$.

Note   *If you took 70% of $2000 (100% − 30%), you would immediately get the cost.*

There is an interesting story about why women wear miniskirts in London, England. It seems that the sales tax is 12.5% on clothes! But children's clothes are tax exempt. A girl's dress is any dress where the skirt is less than 24 inches, so that is why women in London wear miniskirts!

Let's do some problems.

Example 33:

Problems	Solutions
a. Change $\dfrac{3}{4}, \dfrac{5}{8}, 2\dfrac{1}{6}$, and $\dfrac{1}{16}$, to decimals	.75, .625, 2.16666…, .0625
b. Change .3, .24, 3.6, and .026 to (reduced) fractions	$\dfrac{3}{10}, \dfrac{6}{25}, 3\dfrac{3}{5}, \dfrac{13}{500}$
c. Change .456, .32, .6 and 32 to percentages	45.6%, 32 %, 60%, 3200%
d. Change 5%, .4% .07% and 432% to decimals	.05, .004, .0007, 4.32
e. Change 8%, 24%, 220%, .3% to fractions	$\dfrac{2}{25}, \dfrac{6}{25}, \dfrac{11}{5}$ or $2\dfrac{1}{5}, \dfrac{3}{1000}$
f. Change $\dfrac{1}{2}, \dfrac{5}{8}, \dfrac{5}{6}, 2\dfrac{1}{4}$ to percentages	50%, 62.5%, 83.333… or $83\dfrac{1}{3}\%$, 225%,
g. What is 8% of 32?	2.56

h. 14 is what % of 25?   56%

i. 48 is 75% of what number?   64

Example 34: A $40 item is discounted 10%. After a 5% sales tax, the item cost what?

Solution: $37.80.

Example 35: The population decreased from 2400 to 1800. Find the % decrease.

Solution: 600/2400 or 25%

Example 36: On January second, a store advertised a 50% discount, followed by another 50% discount. Did I get it for free?

Solution: No, silly. Suppose an item sells for $100. A 50% discount means you pay $50. Another 50% off means you pay $25. That's why they advertise a 50% discount followed by a 20% discount. It sounds like 70%, but it is really only 60%.

ROUNDING OFF

To round a number off, you need to know two things:

1. What place value you want to round to

2. The value of the digit to the right of that place value

The basic principle is if the digit to the right is less than 5, just replace it and all digits to the right with zeros. If it is 5 or more, add 1 to the digit before, and replace it and all digits to the right with zeros.

Let's take one number and round it off several different ways.

Example 37. Round 4,837 as requested:

Problems	Solutions
To the nearest 10	4,840
To the nearest 100	4,800
To the nearest 1000	5,000

The rules are the same for decimals, except you don't have to fill in the zeros, just drop the numbers to the right of the rounded digit.

Example 38: For the number 37, 543.9873, do the following rounding:

Problems	Solutions
a. To the nearest whole number	Drop 873; 9 > 5; so add 1 to the 3 to get 37,544
b. To the nearest 10	For any number greater than 10, drop off the whole decimal; 3 < 5, so you change it to a 0, to get 37,540
c. To the nearest hundred	4 < 5; fill in with two zeros to get 37,500
d. To the nearest thousand	5 means you add 1 to the digit before and change the 5 and all digits to the right to 0, to get 38,000
e. To the nearest ten thousand	7 > 5, so add 1 to the 9 and change the digits to the right to 0, to get 40,000.
f. To the nearest thousandth	3 is less than 5, so drop it to get 37,543.987
g. To the nearest hundredth	Drop the 3; the 7 is more than 5, so add 1 to the 8, to get 37,543.99
h. To the nearest tenth	Drop the 73; 8 > 5, so add 1 to the 9 to get 37,544.0

Wait a second, aren't parts (a) and (h) the same? No, (h) is more accurate. The point zero means that it is more accurate.

When you see a number like 500 people, you really don't know if that's an exact count or an approximation (a rounded number). If you need to know, ask!

ABSOLUTE VALUE

The **absolute value** of a number is that number (its digits) without a sign, making it always positive.

The sign for absolute value is two parallel lines around the number. So $|3|$ is read as "the absolute value of 3" and its value is 3. Likewise, $|-9| = 9$.

You might ask, "Why did you wait so long to introduce something that is so easy? Absolute value is easy, but it can cause confusion, especially when it is used with letters. Let me show you. What is the value of $|-x|$? The answer is that we need to know the value of x. Luckily, we do not have to deal with this for this test. Whew!

Example 39:   Problems   Solutions

a. What is $|4| + |-4|$? $4 + 4 = 8$

b. What is $-|7| - |7|$? $-7 - 7 = -14$

c. What is $|4| - |7| - |-5|$? $+4 - 7 - 5 = -8$

 Let's do some exercises.

No calculator should be used for these exercises.

Exercise 1: $12 + 1.2 + .12 =$

A. 36   D. 1.44

B. 13.32   E. None of these

C. 2.52

Exercise 2: $37.1 - 3.71 =$

A. 0   D. 34.49

B. 33.39   E. None of these

C. 33.49

Exercise 3: $(.008)(.04) =$

A. 0.02   D. 0.000032

B. 0.0032   E. None of these

C. 0.00032

Exercise 4: $\dfrac{.64}{2000}$

A. 0.000128   D. 0.0032

B. 0.00128   E. None of these

C. 0.00032

Exercise 5: What is 4% of .008?

A. 0.0000032

D. 0.0002

B. 0.000032

E. None of these

C. 0.00032

Exercise 6: 5 is what % of 4?

A. 75%

D. 120%

B. 80%

E. None of these

C. 110%

Exercise 7: 4% of what is 80?

A. 20

D. 320

B. 200

E. None of these

C. 2000

Exercise 8: $\dfrac{3}{4} + \dfrac{5}{6} =$

A. $\dfrac{8}{10}$

D. $\dfrac{19}{12}$

B. $\dfrac{8}{5}$

E. None of these

C. $\dfrac{15}{24}$

Exercise 9: $\dfrac{1}{5} - \dfrac{2}{11} =$

A. $\dfrac{1}{55}$

D. $\dfrac{2}{55}$

B. $\dfrac{21}{55}$

E. None of these

C. $\dfrac{1}{6}$

Exercise 10: $\dfrac{5}{6} \times \dfrac{2}{5}$

    A. $\dfrac{1}{3}$ **D.** $\dfrac{11}{30}$

    B. $\dfrac{2}{5}$ **E.** None of these

    C. $\dfrac{3}{5}$

Exercise 11: $\dfrac{2}{3} \div 4 =$

    A. 6   **D.** $\dfrac{1}{6}$

    B. $\dfrac{8}{3}$ **E.** None of these

    C. $\dfrac{3}{8}$

Exercise 12: 43.998 rounded off to the nearest tenth is

    A. 44.000   **D.** All of these

    B. 44.00   **E.** None of these

    C. 44.0

Exercise 13: (59.9) $\times$ (5.9) is approximately

    A. 10   **D.** 360

    B. 3.6   **E.** None of these

    C. 36

Exercise 14: Reduce $\dfrac{14}{54}$

    A. $\dfrac{1}{4}$ **D.** $\dfrac{4}{9}$

    B. $\dfrac{7}{27}$ **E.** None of these

    C. $\dfrac{1}{3}$

Exercise 15: $4\frac{2}{3}$ as an improper fraction is

A. $\frac{11}{3}$ D. $\frac{66}{3}$

B. $\frac{14}{3}$ E. None of these

C. $\frac{83}{3}$

Exercise 16: $|-7+3|-|-7|+|-3| =$

A. -14 D. 4

B. 24   E. None of these

C. 0

Exercise 17: $5\frac{7}{12} + 4\frac{7}{12} =$

A. $9\frac{14}{26}$ D. $20\frac{1}{6}$

B. $9\frac{1}{6}$ E. None of these

C. $10\frac{1}{6}$

Exercise 18: 50% of $.5 \times \frac{1}{2} =$

A. 1.5   D. 0.125

B. 0.5   E. None of these

C. 0.025

Exercise 19: 123,456 rounded to the nearest thousand is

A. 120,000   D. 123,460

B. 123,000   E. None of these

C. 123,500

Exercise 20: $2\frac{1}{2} \times 2\frac{1}{2}$

      A. $4\frac{1}{4}$ D. $6\frac{1}{4}$

      B. 5   E. None of these

      C. $5\frac{3}{4}$

(A) Let's look at the answers

Answer 1:   B: Align the decimal points and add

Answer 2:   B

Answer 3:   C: $4 \times 8 = 32$, put five decimal places to the left

Answer 4:   C: $\frac{64}{2} = 32$, and insert three more decimal places to the left of .32

Answer 5:   C: $.04 \times .008$

Answer 6:   E: $\frac{5}{4} = 1.25 = 125\%$

Answer 7:   C: $\frac{80}{.04} = \frac{8000}{4}$

Answer 8:   D: $\frac{9}{12} + \frac{10}{12} = \frac{19}{12}$

Answer 9:   A: $\frac{11}{55} - \frac{10}{55} = \frac{1}{55}$

Answer 10:   A: $\frac{10}{30} = \frac{1}{3}$

Answer 11:   D: $\frac{2}{3} \times \frac{1}{4} = \frac{2}{12} = \frac{1}{6}$

Answer 12:   C

Answer 13:   D: about 60×6

Answer 14:   B

Answer 15:   B

Answer 16:   C: $4 - 7 + 3 = -3 + 3 = 0$

Answer 17:   C

Answer 18:   D: $\frac{1}{2} \times \frac{1}{2} \times \frac{1}{2} = \frac{1}{8} = .125$

Answer 19:   B

Answer 20:   D: $\frac{5}{2} \times \frac{5}{2} = \frac{25}{4} = 6\frac{1}{4}$

Let's do a little algebra!

"*Along our journey, we must learn to do. It will help us to become truly happy.*"

Many students I have taught at this level have found that algebra is actually easier than arithmetic. Some have found it much easier. Let's start.

POLYNOMIALS

Let us consider the expression $4x^5 - 7x^3 + 10x^2 + x$. This is a four-term **polynomial**. A polynomial is an expression with numbers and letters and positive integer exponents. A **term** is an expression separated from the next term with a plus sign or a minus sign.

Let's take a look at each term of this polynomial:

$4x^5$: x is the base, 5 is the exponent, and 4 is the **numerical coefficient**. $4x^5 = 4\ xxxxx$ (five factors of x; in algebra, when you indicate multiplication of letters, you just write them next to each other without a multiplication sign). The x is called a **variable**, a letter that stands for a number.

$-7x^3$: x is the base, 3 is the exponent, and -7 is the numerical coefficient. $-7x^3 = (-7)xxx$

$10x^2$: x is the base, 2 is the exponent, and 10 is the numerical coefficient. $10x^2 = 10xx$.

x: x is the same as $1x^1$; the base is x, and the coefficient and exponent are both 1. If it helps, write the 1 for the coefficient and exponent, but most times it is just written as x.

Notes

1. We can also have letter coefficients. If we have the expression am, a is the letter coefficient of m and m is the coefficient of a.

2. For completeness, note that $10x^2$ is not the same as $(10x)^2 = (10x)(10x) = 100x^2$.

LIKE TERMS

Like terms are terms that have the same letter(s), each with the same exponent.

> **Example 1:**   Are these terms like or unlike?

> | Problems | Solutions |
> |---|---|
> | **a.** $4x$ and $-5x$ | Like terms, even though the coefficients are different |
> | **b.** $4x$ and $4xy$ | Unlike terms |
> | **c.** $4x^2y$ and $4xy^2$ | Unlike terms, because the first is $4xxy$ and the second is $4xyy$. |

To **combine** like terms, add or subtract their coefficients. Unlike terms cannot be combined.

> **Example 2:**   Simplify by combining like terms:

> | Problems | Solutions |
> |---|---|
> | **a.** $4x + 3x + 2x$ | $9x$ |
> | **b.** $5x^4 + 3x^4$ | $8x^4$ (exponents don't change) |
> | **c.** $5a + 8b + 3a - 5b$ | $8a + 3b$ |
> | **d.** $4a - 5b - 6a - 7b$ | $-2a - 12b$ |
> | **e.** $6a + 3a + a$ | $10a$ |
> | **f.** $-4a - 5b - 6c - 2a$ | $-6a - 5b - 6c$ |
> | **g.** $a + b + c + d$ | $a + b + c + d$ (no like terms) |

DISTRIBUTIVE LAW

The TABE talks about two distributive laws. The word **distributive** means that whatever coefficient or variable (or both) is in front of any parentheses gets distributed to the terms in the parentheses.

1.   Multiplication is distributed over addition: $a(b + c) = ab + ac$

2.   Multiplication is distributed over subtraction: $a(b - c) = ab - ac$

> **Example 3:**   Multiply, and simplify if necessary

> | Problems | Solutions |
> |---|---|
> | **a.** $4(2x - 5)$ | $8x - 20$ |
> | **b.** $6(x + 5)$ | $6x + 30$ |

c. $-5(2x - 3)$ $-10x + 15$ because $(-5)(-3) = +15$

d. $2(3x + 6) + 5(2x + 1)$ $6x + 12 + 10x + 5 = 16x + 17$

e. $5(x - 5) + 2(2x - 8)$ $5x - 25 + 4x - 16 = 9x - 41$

f. $2(4x - 3) - 5(2x - 6)$ $8x - 6 - 10x + 30 = -2x + 24$

EQUATIONS

The following expressions are all examples of equations.

$$3x + 5 = 7x + 2 \qquad 4x^2 - 7x - 3 = 0 \qquad 4ac + 9x - 3b = 12$$

They have a left side, a right side, and an equal sign in between.

When you think of an equation, you should think of a balance scale with the equal sign being the balance point.

The scale must keep a perfect balance, so if you add something to the left, you must add the same thing to the right. If you subtract something from the right, you must do the same to the left. If you triple the weight on the left, you must triple the weight on the right. Taking half the weight on the right must be followed by taking half the weight on the left to be balanced.

There are four basic one-step equation problems, as shown in the following examples.

Example 4:   Solve for x: $x - 7 = 3$.

Solution: To get a value for x, we want x, or $1x$, to be by itself on the left. We must get rid of the -7. We do that by adding $+7$ to both sides.

$$
\begin{aligned}
x - 7 &= 3 \\
+ 7 &= + 7 \\
x + 0 &= 10 \\
x &= 10
\end{aligned}
$$

To check this solution, substitute 10 for x in the original: $10 - 7 = 3$.

Notes

1. When you are doing this in a math class, you should write in all the steps. When you take the TABE, as soon as you know the answer, choose it, with as few steps as possible. If you know the answer, just choose it.

2. Don't check any question on the TABE until you finish the whole section.

3. The questions will probably be somewhat longer. Notice, we didn't say harder.

Example 5: Solve for x: $x + 7 = 3$

Solution: to get rid of an addition, you subtract or add the negative.

$$x + 7 = 3$$
$$-7 = -7$$

So $x = -4$

This checks because $-4 + 7 = 3$.

Note *The answer can be a negative number; it sometimes is a fraction.*

Example 6: Solve for x: $4x = -23$

Solution: To get rid of a multiplication, use division; in this case, divide each side by 4.

$$4x = -23$$

$$\frac{4x}{4} = \frac{-23}{4}$$

So $1 = x = \dfrac{-23}{4} = -5\dfrac{3}{4}$

Example 7: Solve for x: $\dfrac{x}{-7} = 5$

Solution: To get rid of a division, use multiplication; in this case, multiply both sides by -7.

$$\frac{x}{-7} = 5$$

$$(-7)\left(\frac{x}{-7}\right) (-7)5$$

So $x = -35$

Note *Equations are said to be **equivalent** if they have the same answer; the equations $2x = 6$, $x + 2 = 5$, and $5x + 4 = 19$ are all equivalent because they have the same answer, $x = 3$.*

FIRST-DEGREE EQUATIONS

In high school, the topic of first-degree equations was probably the most popular of all. The TABE asks questions that are not too long and not tricky. The following is a list of steps to get every problem right. After practicing some problems, you will have memorized the steps without trying. Of the problems I've seen, all have less than five steps. The vast majority have two or three.

To solve for x, follow these steps:

1. Multiply by the LCD to get rid of fractions. Cross-multiply if there are only two fractions.
2. If the "x" term appears only on the right, switch the sides.
3. Multiply out all parentheses by using the distributive law.
4. On each side, combine like terms.
5. Add the opposite of the x term on the right to each side.
6. Add the opposite of the non-x term(s) on the left to each side.
7. Divide each side by the whole coefficient of x, including the sign.

Believe it or not, it took a long time to get the phrasing of this list just right.

Note *The **opposite** of a term is the same term with its opposite sign. So the opposite of $3x$ is $-3x$, the opposite of $-7y$ is $+7y$, and the opposite of 0 is 0. The technical name for "opposite" is **additive inverse**.*

Let's do some examples.

Example 8:   Solve for x: $7x - 2 = 10x + 13$

Solution: Steps 1–4 are not present.

$7x - 2 = 10x + 13$ Step 5: Add $-10x$ to each side.
$-3x - 2 = +13$ Step 6: Add $+2$ to each side.
$-3x = 15$ Step 7: Divide each side by -3.
$x = -5$ Solution

Example 9:   Solve for x: $7 = 2(3x - 5) - 4(x - 6)$

Solution:

$7 = 2(3x - 5) - 4(x - 6)$	No Step 1. Step 2: Switch sides.
$2(3x - 5) - 4(x - 6) = 7$	Step 3: Multiply out the parentheses.
$6x - 10 - 4x + 24 = 7$	Step 4: Combine like terms on each side.
$2x + 14 = 7$	No Step 5. Step 6: Add -14 to each side.
$2x = -7$	Step 7: Divide each side by 2.
$x = -\dfrac{7}{2}$	The answer doesn't have to be an integer.

Example 10:   Solve for x: $\dfrac{x}{4} + \dfrac{x}{6} = 1$

Solution:

$\dfrac{x}{4} + \dfrac{x}{6} = 1$	Step 1: Multiply each term by 12.
$3x + 2x = 12$	Step 4: Combine like terms.
$5x = 12$	Step 7: Divide each side by 5.
$x = \dfrac{12}{5}$	Solution

Example 11:   Solve for p: $I = prt$. This is the formula for interest = principal times rate times time.

Solution:

$I = prt$	Step 2: the "x" here is the p term, the letter you solve for.
$prt = I$	Step 7
$\dfrac{prt}{rt} = \dfrac{I}{rt}$	
$p = \dfrac{I}{rt}$	

When you have more than one letter in a problem, you must be given the letter to solve for. We will see this formula again as we work the next examples.

Example 12: $A = \dfrac{1}{2}bh$, solve for h. This formula says that the area of a triangle is one-half the base times the height.

Solution:

$A = \dfrac{1}{2}bh$	Step 1: Multiply both sides by 2.
$2A = bh$	Step 2: Switch sides.
$bh = 2A$	Step 7: Divide both sides by b.
$\dfrac{bh}{b} = \dfrac{2A}{b}$	
$h = \dfrac{2A}{b}$	

Example 13: $p = a + b + c$; solve for c. This formula says that the perimeter of a triangle is found by adding the lengths of the three sides.

Solution:

$p = a + b + c$ Step 2: Switch sides.

$a + b + c = p$ Step 6: Subtract a and b from both sides.

$-a - b = -a - b$

$c = p - a - b$ Remember, you can combine like terms only.

Example 14: Solve for x in each problem.

Problems	Solutions
a. $4x = -40$	-10
b. $\dfrac{x}{5} = 5$	25
c. $x - 9 = -20$	-11
d. $x + 4 = 4$	0
e. $4x + 5x = 18$	2
f. $7x - 9x = 12$	-6
g. $10x = 6x - 20$	-5
h. $4(2x - 5) = 7$	$\dfrac{27}{8}$
i. $2(2x - 5) = 4(2x - 3)$	$\dfrac{1}{2}$
j. $2x + 5 + x + 7 = 18$	2
k. $\dfrac{x}{3} + \dfrac{x}{4} = 7$	12
l. $ax = 7$	$\dfrac{7}{a}$
m. $wxy + 6 = a$	$\dfrac{a - 6}{wy}$
n. $2ax - 3a = 7a$	$\dfrac{10a}{2a} = 5$
o. $2x + \dfrac{1}{2}x = 10$	4
p. $-3(2x - 6) = 11$	$\dfrac{7}{6}$
q. $2x + 3 + 4 + 5x = 0$	-1
r. $9x - 9 = -9$	0

INEQUALITIES

To review some facts about inequalities:

$a < b$ (read as "a is less than b") means a is to the left of b on the number line.

$a > b$ (read as "a is greater than b") means a is to the right of b on the number line.

$x > y$ is the same as $y < x$.

The notation $x \geq y$ (read as "x is greater than or equal to y") means $x > y$ or $x = y$. $9 \geq 4$ because $9 > 4$; $7 \geq 7$ because $7 = 7$; however, $2 \geq 4$ is not true because $2 < 4$.

Similarly, $x \leq y$ (read as "x is less than or equal to y") means $x < y$ or $x = y$.

We solve inequalities the same way we solve equalities, except when we multiply or divide by a negative, the order of the inequality reverses. Let us see why.

If $8 < 10$, then $8 + 2 < 10 + 2$, $8 - 2 < 10 - 2$, $8(2) < 10(2)$, and $8/2 < 10/2$. So if we add, subtract, multiply by a positive, or divide by a positive, the order remains the same. B-u-u-u-u-t, let us see what happens if we multiply and divide by negatives.

$8 < 10$, but $8(-2) > 10(-2)$, because $-16 > -20$. If you were dealing with money, losing 16 dollars wouldn't be as bad as losing 20 dollars. Also, $\frac{8}{-2} > \frac{10}{-2}$ because $-4 > -5$.

I mentioned above that losing 16 dollars is not as bad as losing 20—the more you are negative, the worse off you are. However, that is not entirely true. Take the case of Mr. William Randolph Hearst. Early in the twentieth century, Mr. Hearst had a gigantic publishing empire (you should read about him). He had hundreds of millions of dollars at a time when a hundred million was worth more than ten billion in today's dollars (and there was no income tax at the time!). But then he fell on some bad times. The banks could tell him what he could or could not do. He wanted to build a mansion. The banks wouldn't let him. He was furious! What he didn't tell the public is that he still owned seven mansions, and he was one hundred million dollars in debt! (But he was still rich.) It is because of the golden rule. Those who have the gold, rule (and make up laws to benefit themselves).

Example 15: Solve for x: $6x + 2 < 3x + 10$

Solution: $3x < 8$, so $x < \frac{8}{3}$.

The inequality does not switch because both sides are divided by a positive number (3).

Example 16: Solve for x: $-2(x - 3) \leq 4x - 3 - 7$

Solution: $-2x + 6 \leq 4x - 10$, or $-6x \leq -16$. Thus, $x \geq \dfrac{-16}{-6} = \dfrac{8}{3}$.

Here the inequality switches because we divided both sides by a negative number (-6).

Example 17: Solve for x: $3x + 4y > 5$

Solution:

$3x + 4y > 5$ 　　　　　　Subtract 4y from both sides

$3x > 5 - 4y$ 　　　　　　Divide by 3

$x > \dfrac{5}{3} - \dfrac{4y}{3}$, or $x > \left(\dfrac{-4}{3}\right)y + \dfrac{5}{3}$, or $x > \dfrac{-4}{3}(y) + \dfrac{5}{3}$

Example 18: Solve for x:

Problems	Solutions
a. $3x < 12$	$x < 4$
b. $-3x \leq 14$	$x \geq -\dfrac{14}{3}$
c. $\dfrac{x}{6} > 6$	$x > 36$
d. $\dfrac{x}{(-2)} < 5$	$x > -10$
e. $x + 6 < 2$	$x < -4$
f. $2x + 5 \leq -7$	$x \leq -6$
g. $-3x + 5 < 11$	$x > -2$
h. $\dfrac{x}{3} + 5 < 7$	$x < 6$
i. $2x + 5 < 4x + 3$	$x > 1$
j. $x + 6 \leq 4x + 11$	$x \geq -\dfrac{5}{3}$
k. $5x - 7y < 35$	$x < \left(\dfrac{7}{5}\right)y + 7$
l. $-2x + 4y \leq 8$	$x \geq 2y - 4$ or $2y + {}^-4$

EVEN MORE ON THE LAWS OF EXPONENTS

The TABE asks questions on exponents with letter bases. Most of my students think this is a lot easier than number bases because the arithmetic is much less or even zero. The rules for exponents listed in Chapter 1 work for both number and letter bases. The rules for letter bases are repeated here.

Rule	Examples
1. $x^m x^n = x^{m+n}$	$x^6 x^4 x = x^{11}$ and $(x^6 y^7)(x^4 y^{10}) = x^{10} y^{17}$
2. $\dfrac{x^m}{n^n} = x^{m-n} = \dfrac{1}{x^{n-m}}$	$\dfrac{x^8}{x^6} = x^2$, $\dfrac{x^3}{x^7} = \dfrac{1}{x^4}$ and $\dfrac{x^4 y^5 z^9}{x^9 y^2 z^9} = \dfrac{y^3}{x^5}$
3. $(x^m)^n = x^{mn}$	$(x^5)^7 = x^{35}$
4. $(xy)^n = x^n y^n$	$(xy)^3 = x^3 y^3$ and $(x^7 y^3)^{10} = x^{70} y^{30}$
5. $\left(\dfrac{x}{y}\right)^n = \dfrac{x^n}{y^n}$	$\left(\dfrac{x}{y}\right)^6 = \dfrac{x^6}{y^6}$ and $\left(\dfrac{y^4}{z^5}\right)^3 = \dfrac{y^{12}}{z^{15}}$

You should also recall the following:

Rule	Examples
6. $x^{-n} = \dfrac{1}{x^n}$ and $\dfrac{1}{x^{-m}} = x^m$	$2^{-3} = \dfrac{1}{2^3} = \dfrac{1}{8}$, $\dfrac{1}{4^{-3}} = 4^3 = 64$,
	$\dfrac{x^{-4} y^{-5} z^6}{x^{-6} y^4 z^{-1}} = \dfrac{x^6 z^6 z^1}{x^4 y^5 y^4} = \dfrac{x^2 z^7}{y^9}$,
	and $\left(\dfrac{x^3}{y^{-4}}\right)^{-2} = \left(\dfrac{y^{-4}}{x^3}\right)^2 = \dfrac{y^{-8}}{x^6} = \dfrac{1}{x^6 y^8}$
7. $x^0 = 1, x \neq 0$; 0^0 is indeterminate	$(7ab)^0 = 1$ and $7x^0 = 7(1) = 7$

The following example includes a little more than may be needed, but I am afraid of leaving out something the TABE may ask.

Example 19: Simplify these problems. Your answers should have no negative exponents.

Problems	Solutions
a. $(2x^5)(6x^3)$	$12x^8$
b. $\dfrac{8x^7}{2x^5}$	$4x^2$

c. $\dfrac{6x^3}{10x^5}$ $\qquad\qquad\qquad\qquad$ $\dfrac{3}{5x^2}$

d. $(4x^3yz^5)^3$ $\qquad\qquad\qquad$ $(4^1x^3y^1z^5)^3 = 4^{1(3)}x^{3(3)}y^{1(3)}z^{5(3)}) = 64x^9y^3z^{15}$

e. x^{-3} $\qquad\qquad\qquad\qquad\qquad$ $\dfrac{1}{x^3}$

f. $\dfrac{1}{5x^{-4}}$ $\qquad\qquad\qquad\qquad$ $\dfrac{x^4}{5}$

g. $\dfrac{x^{-5}}{y^{-6}}$ $\qquad\qquad\qquad\qquad$ $\dfrac{y^6}{x^5}$

h. $(-3a^4bc^6)(-5ab^7c^{10})$ $\qquad$ $-1500a^{105}b^{208}c^{2016}$
    $(-100a^{100}b^{200}c^{2000})$

i. $(10ab^4c^7)^3$ $\qquad\qquad\qquad$ $1000a^3b^{12}c^{21}$

j. $(4x^6)^2(10x^3)^3$ $\qquad\qquad$ $16000x^{21}$

k. $((2b^4)^3)^2$ $\qquad\qquad\qquad$ $64b^{24}$

l. $(-b^6)^{101}$ $\qquad\qquad\qquad$ $-b^{606}$

m. $(-ab^8)^{202}$ $\qquad\qquad\qquad$ $1a^{202}b^{1616}$

n. $\dfrac{24e^9f^7g^5}{72e^9f^{11}g^7} =$ $\qquad\qquad$ $\dfrac{1}{3f^4g^2}$

o. $\dfrac{(x^4)^3}{x^4}$ $\qquad\qquad\qquad\qquad$ x^8

p. $\left(\dfrac{m^3n^4}{m^7n}\right)^5 =$ $\qquad\qquad$ $\dfrac{n^{15}}{m^{20}}$

q. $\left(\dfrac{(p^4)^3}{(p^6)^5}\right)^{10} =$ $\qquad\qquad$ $\dfrac{1}{p^{180}}$

r. $(-10a^{-4}b^5c^{-2})(4a^{-7}b^{-1}) =$ $\qquad$ $\dfrac{-40b^4}{a^{11}c^2}$

s. $(3ab^{-3}c^4)^{-3} =$ $\qquad\qquad$ $\dfrac{b^9}{27a^3c^{12}}$

t. $(3x^{-4})\left(\dfrac{3^{-1}x^6}{x^2}\right)$ $\qquad\qquad$ 1

u. $(2x^{-4})^2(3x^{-3})^{-2} =$ $\qquad\qquad$ $\dfrac{4}{9x^2} =$

v. $\left(\dfrac{(2y^3)^{-2}}{4x^{-5}}\right)^{-2} =$ $\qquad\qquad$ $\dfrac{256y^{12}}{x^{10}}$

Let's do some exercises.

No calculator should be used for these exercises.

Exercise 1:   In the expression $3x^6 - 5x^2 + 4$, -5 is the

    A. Base   D. Degree

    B. Exponent   E. None of these

    C. Numerical Coefficient

Exercise 2:   In $7x^3$, the 3 is called a(n)

    A. Power   D. All of these

    B. Exponent   E. None of these

    C. Cube

Exercise 3: $-5x$ and $2x$ are called

    A. Like terms   D. Functions

    B. Unlike terms   E. None of these

    C. Equations

Exercise 4:   Combine $-5x + 2x$

    A. $-3x$ D. Cannot be combined

    B. $-7x$ E. None of these

    C. $-10x^2$

Exercise 5:   Simplifying $4x + 5y - 6x - 2y$ gives

    A. $-2x - 3y$ D. $17xy$

    B. $-2x + 3y$ E. None of these

    C. $2x + 3y$

Exercise 6:   Multiply: $4(3x - 4y - 6)$. The answer is

A. $12x - 4y - 6$ D. $-288xy$

B. $12x - 16y - 6$ E. None of these

C. $12x - 16y - 24$

Exercise 7:   Simplified, $4(x - 5) - 3(2x - 6)$ is

A. $2x + 2$ D. $-2x - 38$

B. $-2x + 2$ E. None of these

C. $-2x - 2$

Exercise 8:   Simplified, $4x^3 + 7x^3 + x^3$ is

A. $12x^3$ D. $11x^9$

B. $11x^3$ E. None of these

C. $12x^9$

Exercise 9: $\dfrac{x}{6} = 6; x =$

A. 0   D. 36

B. 1   E. None of these

C. 6

Exercise 10: $x - 7 = -9 ; x =$

A. -16 D. 16

B. -2 E. None of these

C. 2

Exercise 11: $2x - 7 = 17; x =$

A. 5   D. -12

B. 12   E. None of these

C. 119/2

Exercise 12: $3x - 5 = 8x - 5; x =$

    A. -1 **D.** -5

    B. 0 **E.** None of these

    C. 1

Exercise 13: If $x - 5 < 6$, then

    A. $x > 11$ **D.** $x < 30$

    B. $x > 30$ **E.** None of these

    C. $x < 11$

Exercise 14: $-3x > 21;$

    A. $x > 18$ **D.** $x < -7$

    B. $x < 18$ **E.** None of these

    C. $x > -7$

Exercise 15: If $x - a = m$, then $x =$

    A. $a + m$ **D.** $-am$

    B. $m - a$ **E.** None of these

    C. am

Exercise 16: If $ax + b = c$, then $x =$

    A. $c - b - a$ **D.** $-abc$

    B. $c - b + a$ **E.** None of these

    C. $\dfrac{c - b}{a}$

Exercise 17: If $3x - 6y > 12$, then

    A. $x > 2y + 4$ **D.** $x > -2y - 4$

    B. $x > -2y + 4$ **E.** None of these

    C. $x > 2y - 4$

Exercise 18: $(4x^3y^5)(-3x^6y^7) =$

  A. x^9y^{12} D. Can't be multiplied

  B. $-12x^9y^{12}$ E. None of these

  C. $-12x^{18}y^{35}$

Exercise 19: $\dfrac{3x^{-3}}{5y^{-5}} =$

  A. $\dfrac{15y^5}{x^3}$ D. $\dfrac{y^5}{15x^3}$

  B. $\dfrac{3y^5}{5x^3}$ E. None of these

  C. $\dfrac{5y^5}{3x^3}$

Exercise 20: Simplified, $(4x^{-6})(5x^7)(x)$ is

  A. $20x$ D. 102

  B. $20x^2$ E. None of these

  C. $1024x$

(A) Let's look at the answers

Answer 1:   C

Answer 2:   D

Answer 3:   A: Like terms are not determined by the sign of the coefficient

Answer 4:   A

Answer 5:   B: $4x - 6x = -2x$ and $5y - 2y = 3y$; use the sign of the larger number without the sign

Answer 6:   C: 6 multiplies each term in the parentheses

Answer 7:   C: $4x - 20 - 6x + 18 = -2x - 2$

Answer 8:   A: $x^3 = 1x^3$; add the coefficients, but the base and exponents stay the same

Answer 9:   D: Multiply each side by 6

Answer 10:   B: Add $+7$ to each side

Answer 11:   B: Add $+7$ to each side; then divide by 2

Answer 12:   B: Add 5 to each side; divide both sides by -5; $\dfrac{0}{-5} = 0$

Answer 13:   C: Add 5 to each side; order doesn't change

Answer 14:   D: Divide by -3; order changes

Answer 15:   A: Add a to both sides

Answer 16:   C: Subtract b from both sides; then divide both sides by a

Answer 17:   A: Add $6y$ to each side, and then divide by 3

Answer 18:   B: Multiply coefficients; add the exponents

Answer 19:   B: The letters change location because of the negative exponents, but the numbers don't

Answer 20:   B: $x = 1x^1$; multiply the coefficients (4)(5)(1) and add the exponents, $-6 + 7 + 1 = 2$.

CHAPTER 5: *Words and Problems with Words*

"*It is necessary to study the words of math. Only then can you truly understand all.*"

Many of the TABE questions are in words, not just numbers, and you have to know how to read these "word problems" to be able to solve them. Fortunately, there are usually only a small number of words. That means each word is very, very important. You must know them. This is also very important in the real world. The boss (hopefully, you someday) will sometimes give you a sheet of paper with instructions for what to do. If you can do them quickly, well, and profitably, you will get promoted with big raises. We will do some examples to help you conquer word problems here.

Okay, let's get started!!!!!

BASICS

As we have seen, the answer in **addition** is the **sum**. Other words that indicate addition are **plus**, **more**, **more than**, **increase**, and **increased by**. You can write all sums in any order.

The answer in **multiplication** is the **product**. Another word that is used is **times**. Sometimes the word **of** indicates multiplication, as we shall see shortly. **Double** means to multiply by two, and **triple** means to multiply by three. We can also write any product in any order.

Division's answer is called the **quotient**. Another phrase that is used is **divided by**.

The answer in **subtraction** is called the **difference**. Subtraction can present a reading problem because $4 - 6 \neq 6 - 4$, so we must be careful to subtract in the correct order. The following list shows how some subtraction phrases are translated into number problems and algebraic expressions involving subtraction.

Phrases	Translations
1. The difference between 9 and 5	$9 - 5$
The difference between m and n	$m - n$
2. Five minus two	$5 - 2$
m minus n	$m - n$
3. Seven decreased by three	$7 - 3$
m decreased by n	$m - n$
4. Nine diminished by four	$9 - 4$
m diminished by n	$m - n$
5. Three from five	$5 - 3$
m from n	$n - m$
6. Ten less two	$10 - 2$
m less n	$m - n$
7. Ten less than two	$2 - 10$
m less than n	$n - m$

Notice in the last four phrases how one word makes a difference: a less b means $a - b$, but a less *than* b means $b - a$. In addition, we have seen that a *is* less than b means $a < b$. You must read carefully!

The following words usually indicate an equal sign: *is, am, are, was, were, the same as, equal to*.

You also must know the symbols for the following phrases:

1. *More than* or *over* is $>$
2. *At least* is $\geq$
3. *Less than* or *under* means $<$
4. *At most* is $\leq$

Example 1:   Write the following phrases in symbols:

Problems	Solutions
a. m times the sum of q and r	$m(q + r)$
b. Six less the product of x and y	$6 - xy$

c. The difference between
c and d divided by f
$$\frac{c-d}{f}$$

d. b less than the quotient
of r divided by s
$$\frac{r}{s} - b$$

e. The sum of d and g is the
same as the product of
h and r
$$d + g = hr$$

f. x is at least y
$$x \geq y$$

g. Zeb's age n is not more
than 21
$$n \leq 21$$

h. I am over 30 years old
$$I > 30$$

i. Most people are under
seven feet tall
$$p < 7$$

Note *The word* number *does not necessarily mean an integer or even necessarily a positive number.*

DISTANCE, SPEED, AND TIME

Very common problems found in the real world and the not-so-real math books are those that involve distance, speed, and time.

If we go 30 miles per hour for four hours, we travel 120 miles. In symbols,

$$d = r \times t$$

In words, the distance d = the rate (speed), r, times the time, t.

Note *Because $d = r \times t$, we can also say the rate $r = \frac{d}{t}$, and the time $t = \frac{d}{r}$.*

Example 2: A car leaves at 3:30 p.m. and arrives at its destination, 270 miles away, at 8:00 p.m. the same day. Find its speed.

Solution: $r - \frac{d}{t} = \frac{270 \text{ miles}}{4.5 \text{ hours}} = 60$ miles per hour (mph).

Note *60 miles per hour = 1 mile per minute. On a highway that has mile markers, and if you go at 60 mph, it should take you exactly 1 minute between markers. You can check how accurate your speedometer is. Try it!*

Example 3:   If you travel 400 miles in 8 hours, what is your average speed?

Solution: $r = \dfrac{d}{t} = \dfrac{400}{8} = 50$ mph.

RATIOS

Comparing two numbers is called a **ratio**. The ratio of 3 to 5 is written two ways: $\dfrac{3}{5}$ or 3:5 (read as "the ratio of 3 to 5").

Example 4:   Find the ratio of 5 ounces to 2 pounds.

Solution: The ratio is $\dfrac{5}{32}$ because 16 ounces are in a pound.

Example 5:   A board is cut into two pieces that are in the ratio of 3 to 4. If the board is 56 inches long, how long is the longer piece?

Solution: If the pieces are in the ratio 3:4, we let one piece equal $3x$ and the other $4x$. The equation, then, is $3x + 4x = 56$; so $x = 8$; and the longer piece is $4x = 32$ inches.

I have asked this problem many, many times. Almost no one has ever gotten it correct—not because it is difficult, but because no one does problems like this one anymore.

PROPORTION

A proportion is two ratios equal to each other.

For example, $\dfrac{4}{6} = \dfrac{10}{15}$ because they both reduce to $\dfrac{2}{3}$.

Notice that if we multiply the top of one ratio by the bottom of the other, the product is the same as multiplying the other top and bottom. That is called **cross-multiplication** and it is always true in a proportion. So in the proportion above, $4(15) = 6(10)$.

In symbols, if $\dfrac{a}{b} = \dfrac{c}{d}$, then $ad = bc$. Cross-multiplication is the quickest way to solve a proportion.

Example 6:   Solve for x if $\dfrac{x}{12} = \dfrac{7}{4}$.

Solution: Solving, we get $4x = 84$; so $x = \dfrac{84}{4} = 21$.

Example 7:   If 12 oranges cost \$1.80, how much do 18 oranges cost?

Solution: Let $x =$ cost of 18 oranges. We set up the proportion $\dfrac{\text{cost}}{\text{oranges}} = \dfrac{\text{cost}}{\text{oranges}}$.

Then $\dfrac{\$1.80}{12} = \dfrac{x}{18}$. Solving, we get $12x = 18(\$1.80) = 32.40$; so $x = \dfrac{\$32.40}{12} = \$2.70$.

Example 8:   A recipe calls for $\dfrac{1}{4}$ teaspoon of salt for every $1\dfrac{1}{2}$ cups of flour. How much salt is needed for 15 cups of flour?

Solution: We let $x =$ the number of teaspoons of salt. The proportion we set up is $\dfrac{\text{teaspoons}}{\text{cups}} = \dfrac{\text{teaspoons}}{\text{cups}}$. Changing $1\dfrac{1}{2}$ cups to $\dfrac{3}{2}$ cups, we get $\dfrac{\frac{1}{4}}{\frac{3}{2}} = \dfrac{x}{15}$, or

$$\dfrac{3}{2}x = (15)\left(\dfrac{1}{4}\right) = \dfrac{15}{4}.$$

If we multiply the equation $\dfrac{3}{2}x = \dfrac{15}{4}$ by 4, the LCD, we get $6x = 15$. Dividing each side by 6, we get $x = \dfrac{15}{6} = 2\dfrac{1}{2}$ teaspoons of salt.

Tipping

Example 9:   At a fancy restaurant, tipping is usually 25% (not so fancy, it is 15% or 20%). What do you pay on a \$360 dinner?

Solution: Take \$360 and multiply it by .25 (or $\dfrac{1}{4}$), and get \$90. The total meal cost would be \$360 + \$90 = \$450, a lot of money for a meal.

Example 10:   A meal, including a 20% tip, cost \$48. What was the cost of the meal before the tip?

Solution: A 20% tip means 120% of the cost of the meal was \$48. If $x =$ the cost of the meal, we have (remember that 120% = 1.2) $1.2x = 48$; $x = \dfrac{48}{1.2} = \$40$.

Note *On this part of the test, you can use a calculator. The numbers may be a lot messier than in these problems.*

Discounts and Markups in Retail Businesses

Example 11: A $64 sweater was discounted 20%. How much did the sweater cost?

Solution:

Method 1: $64 × .20 = $12.80 discount. $64 − $12.80 = $51.20.
Method 2: A 20% discount means you are paying 100% − 20% = 80% of the cost. $64 × .80 = $51.20.

Example 12: The wholesale price of a coat is $80. The store marks it up 75%. How much do you pay?

Solution: $80 × .75 = $60. The coat would cost you $80 + $60 = $140.

Note *This may seem like a lot, but businesses must earn a profit. If they don't, everyone loses their jobs.*

Example 13: A jacket that wholesales for $75 sells for $175. What is the percentage markup?

Solution: The markup is $175 − $75 = $100. The percentage markup is

$$\frac{\$100}{\$75} = 133\frac{1}{3}\%.$$

Note *Very important! Percentage markups and percentage discounts are always on the original price.*

Example 14: A January after-holiday sale has a store selling an $80 jacket for a 50% discount followed by a 20% discount. How much do you pay?

Solution: 50% ($\frac{1}{2}$) of $80 = $40. Another 20% of means you pay 80% of $40 = .8(40) = $32. The discount was $80 − $32 = $48, so the percentage discount was $\frac{\$48}{\$80}$ = 60%.

You may ask, why didn't the store just say a 70% discount? The reason the store said 50% followed by 20% is that it sounds like 70% but is really only 60%. Buyer beware! To put it another way, if a store offers a 50% discount followed by another 50%, do you really think you get it for free?! (It actually is a 75% discount.)

MISCELLANEOUS PROBLEMS

Sometimes the TABE gives you a formula, real or not. Then, from the information you have, you must follow the directions of the problem and solve it. You do not have to understand it. You just have to find the answer.

Example 15: The gravitational pull between two planets is directly proportional to a constant times the product of the masses and is inversely proportional to the square of the distance between them. Its formula is given by $F = 1,000,000 \times \dfrac{M \times N}{d^2}$, where M and N are the masses of the planets, and d is the distance between them. If $M = 200$, $N = 1600$, and $d = 400$, find F.

Solution: You really don't have to know what gravitational pull is or even what *directly proportional* or *inversely proportional* mean. You just need to know the formula and the values of the variables, which are all given to you.

$$F = 1,000,000 \times \frac{200 \times 1600}{400 \times 400} = 2,000,000$$

Note *You might have been able to do this problem without a calculator by canceling a lot of the zeros on the top with zeros on the bottom. However, because calculators can be used on this part of the TABE, the calculations can sometimes be really messy.*

Example 16: A $60 shirt is discounted 20%. How much do you pay?

Solution: $60 \times .80 = $48.00.

Example 17: If you go 500 miles in 8 hours, what is your average speed?

Solution: $\dfrac{500}{8} = 62.5$ miles per hour.

Example 18:   If CDs are 4 for $34, how much do 10 CDs cost?

Solution: Let x = cost of 10 CDs. We get $\dfrac{34}{4} = \dfrac{x}{10}$. By cross-multiplying, we get $4x = 340$; $x = \$85.00$.

Example 19:   A $40 used textbook is 75% less than a new one. How much does the new one cost?

Solution: If the book is 75% less than the new one, it is 25% of the new one costing x dollars. The equation is $.25x = \$40$; $x = \$160.00$.

Example 20:   A truck goes 2 hours at 40 mph and 3 hours at 60 mph. What is the average speed?

Solution: Average speed $= \dfrac{\text{total distance}}{\text{total time}}$. The total time is $2 + 3 = 5$ hours. To find the total distance, add $40 \times 2 = 80$ miles and $3 \times 60 = 180$ miles. So $r = \dfrac{260}{5} = 52$ mph.

Example 21:   A car goes 279 miles on 9 gallons of gas. How many miles per gallon does it get?

Solution: *Per* means divide! $\dfrac{279}{9} = 31$ miles per gallon. Good fuel efficiency!

Example 22:   A necklace that wholesales for $150 is priced at $240. What is the store's percentage markup?

Solution: The markup is $\$240 - \$150 = \$90$. The percentage markup is thus $\dfrac{90}{150} = .60 = 60\%$ markup.

Example 23:   You bought 20 shares of company XYZ at $30 per share. Two years later, you sold it at $900. What was your percentage profit?

Solution: $20 \times 30 = \$600$ cost. $\$900 - \$600 = \$300$ profit. So the percentage profit is $\dfrac{300}{600} = 50\%$.

Example 24:   A meal cost $60. If there is a 5% sales tax, and if you decide to leave a tip of 20% of the total including tax, how much do you pay?

Solution: $.05 \times \$60 = \$3$ tax. $\$60 + \$3 = \$63$. $\$63 \times .20 = \$12.60$ tip. So $\$63 + \$12.60 = \$75.60$ is what you pay.

Example 25: On a minor league baseball team, the star gets 3 hits every 8 at-bats. If the star has 512 at-bats, how many hits will he get?

Solution: Let x = number of hits in 512 at-bats. Then the proportion is $\frac{3}{8} = \frac{x}{512}$. By cross-multiplying, we get $8x = 1536$; $x = 192$ hits. Anyone in the majors doing this over a career would be in the Baseball Hall of Fame because this is higher than the highest there now.

Example 26: At 2 p.m., you leave one city, arriving at another city at 6:30 p.m. the same day. If you travel 360 miles, what is your average speed?

Solution: $\frac{360}{4.5} = 80$ mph.

 Let's do some exercises.

Calculators are permitted for these exercises.

Exercise 1: "Four less than a number x is 6 less twice the same number" can be exactly written

    A. $x - 4 = 2x - 6$ **C.** $4 - x = 2x - 6$

    B. $x - 4 = 6 - 2x$ **D.** $4 - x = 6 - 2x$

Exercise 2: "y is at least 4 more than twice x" is written

    A. $y > 2x + 4$ **C.** $y \geq 2x + 4$

    B. $y < 2x + 4$ **D.** $y \leq 2x + 4$

Exercise 3: Rate times time is the distance. Going 2000 miles in 6 hours gives an average rate in miles per hour of

    A. 1994   **C.** 2004

    B. 12000   **D.** 333.3

Exercise 4: Simple interest is principal times rate times time. If the principal is $2000 and the interest rate is 6% a year, how much money will you have in $2\frac{1}{2}$ years?

A. $300   C. $3000

B. $2300   D. $5000

Exercise 5: The volume of a sphere is $V = \frac{4}{3}\pi r^3$, where r is the radius. If $\pi = \frac{22}{7}$ and the diameter is 24, then the volume is

A. 7238.2   C. 7241.1

B. 57905.8   D. 57929.1

Exercise 6: A house valued at $11,000 is assessed, for real estate purposes, at $2.20 per hundred dollars assessment per year. The real estate taxes are

A. $24.20   C. $2420

B. $242   D. $24,200

Exercise 7: If $\frac{x}{24} = \frac{7}{3}$, $x =$

A. 56   C. 336

B. 168   D. less than 1

Exercise 8: If $\frac{2x}{45} = \frac{8}{15}$, $x =$

A. 6   C. 12

B. 9   D. 240

Exercise 9: If 10 oranges cost $2.40, then 15 oranges cost

A. $1.20   C. $4.80

B. $3.60   D. $36.00

Exercise 10: You were charged $44 for a sweater, which was 80% of the original cost. The original cost was

      A. $35.20   **C.** $55

      B. $33   **D.** $99

Exercise 11: You drove a car valued at $26,000 off the showroom floor. Its value immediately decreased by 25%. Its new value was

      A. $19,500   **C.** $21,000

      B. $20,500   **D.** $30,000

Exercise 12: An 18% gratuity is added to a food bill of $120. The total bill is

      A. $21.60   **C.** $141.60

      B. $98.40   **D.** $160

Exercise 13: A car is driven 260 miles on 7 gallons of gas. The mileage in mph is about

      A. 25   **C.** 37

      B. 32   **D.** 1840

Exercise 14: A 72-foot board is divided in the ratio of 2 to 3 to 4. The largest piece is

      A. 16   **C.** 32

      B. 24   **D.** 40

Exercise 15: A basketball player hits 92% of her free throws. If she attempts 250, how many did she make?

      A. 220   **C.** 232

      B. 230   **D.** 236

Exercise 16: A stock increased from $60 to $70 a share. The percentage increase was

      A. 10   **C.** $16\frac{2}{3}$

      B. $14\frac{2}{7}$ **D.** 20

Exercise 17: A stock decreased from $60 to $50 a share. The percentage decrease was

A. 10   C. $16\frac{2}{3}$

B. 15   D. 20

Exercise 18: A used book is 14% of the cost of a new book. If the new cost is $80, the used cost is

A. $66   C. $20.20

B. $54   D. $11.20

Exercise 19: You drive 2 hours at 40 mph and 3 hours at 60 mph. Your total mileage is

A. 160   C. 300

B. 260   D. 360

Exercise 20: You have at most $100 to spend. One item you buy costs $15. How many $10 items can you buy?

A. 7   C. 9

B. 8   D. 10

 Let's look at the answers

Answer 1:   B: *Less than* reverses; *less* does not.

Answer 2:   C: *At least* means that amount or more, greater than or equal to.

Answer 3:   D: $\dfrac{2000}{6} = 333.3$.

Answer 4:   B: The interest is $300. The total is $2000 + $300 = $2300.

Answer 5:   C: The radius $= \dfrac{24}{2} = 12$. You must use $\pi = \dfrac{22}{7}$. You cannot use the π on the calculator because the problem says to use their value!

$$\left(\frac{4}{3}\right)\left(\frac{22}{7}\right)(12^3) \approx 7241.1$$

Answer 6: B: $2.20 per hundred; $22 per thousand; $22 × 11 = $242 for $11,000.

Answer 7: A: By cross-multiplying, we get $3x = (24)(7)$, so $x = \dfrac{168}{3} = 56$.

Answer 8: C: By cross-multiplying, we get $2(15x) = 8(45)$; $x = \dfrac{360}{30} = 12$.

Answer 9: B: 5 oranges cost $1.20; so 15 oranges cost $3.60; or use $\dfrac{\$240}{10} = \dfrac{x}{15}$.

Answer 10: C: $\dfrac{44}{.80} = \$55$.

Answer 11: A: $26,000 − (.25)26,000. A new car loses a lot of value the second you drive it home!

Answer 12: C: $120 + .18(120) = $141.60.

Answer 13: C: $\dfrac{260}{7} \approx 37$.

Answer 14: C: $2x + 3x + 4x = 72$; $9x = 72$; $x = 8$; the largest piece is $4x$, or $4(8) = 32$.

Answer 15: B: 250 × .92 = 230.

Answer 16: C: $70 − 60 = 10$; $\dfrac{10}{60} \times 100\% = 16\dfrac{2}{3}\%$.

Answer 17: C: $60 − 50 = 10$; $\dfrac{10}{60} \times 100\% = 16\dfrac{2}{3}\%$.

Answer 18: D: $80 × .14. It is m-u-u-u-u-u-ch cheaper to buy used books.

Answer 19: B: $(2 \times 40) + (3 \times 60) = 260$.

Answer 20: B: $10x + 15 \le 100$; $10x \le 85$; so $x \le 8.5$. However, you cannot buy half an item, so the answer is 8.

CHAPTER 6: *Geometry Basics*

"*Your journey began from a single point. You travel in a straight line; sometimes the slope may be steep and the distance seems far, but you are now at the midpoint. The endpoint is in sight.*"

At the beginning of each new area of math, we need to explain a few terms.

Point: We all know what a point is. Knowing what a point is makes understanding the other terms easier.

Line: We mean a straight line that goes on forever.

Line Segment: All points on a line between two points including the endpoints.

Ray: All points on one side of a point on a line, including that point (the **endpoint**).

The notation for this ray is $\overrightarrow{AB}$. *A* is the endpoint.

Angle: Two rays with a common endpoint, called the **vertex**.

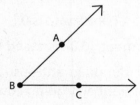

This angle is written as ∠*ABC*, or ∠*CBA*, or, when there is no confusion, ∠*B*.

B is the vertex here. When you read an angle with three letters, the vertex is *always* in the middle.

Okay, okay, enough words (for now). Let's get started.

POINTS IN THE PLANE

We start with a **plane**—a two-dimensional space, like a piece of paper. On this plane, we draw two perpendicular lines, or **axes**. The x-axis is horizontal; the y-axis is vertical. Positive x is to the right; negative x is to the left. Positive y is up; negative y is down. Points in the plane are indicated by **ordered pairs** (x, y). The x number, called the **first coordinate** or **abscissa**, is always given first; the y number, called the **second coordinate** or **ordinate**, is always given second. Here are some points on the plane.

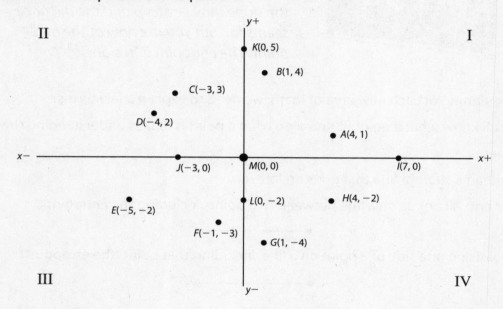

Note the following:

- For any point on the x-axis, the y coordinate is always 0.
- For any point on the y-axis, the x coordinate is 0.
- The point where the two axes meet, (0,0), is called the **origin**.
- The axes divide the plane into four quadrants, usually written with roman numerals, starting in the upper right quadrant and going counterclockwise.

    In quadrant I, x > 0 and y > 0.

    In quadrant II, x < 0 and y > 0.

    In quadrant III, x < 0 and y < 0.

    In quadrant IV, x > 0 and y < 0.

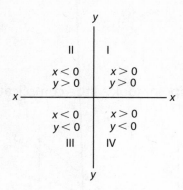

In the following figure, we draw the line $y = x$. For every point on this line, the first coordinate has the same value as the second coordinate, or $y = x$. If we shade the area above this line, all of the points in the shaded portion have y values that are larger than the x values, or $y > x$ in the shaded portion. Similarly, $x > y$ in the unshaded portion. Sometimes, questions on the TABE ask about this.

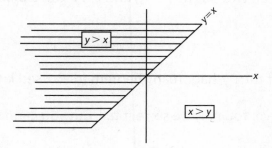

The following figure shows **symmetry** about the x-axis, y-axis, and the origin. If you folded the paper on a line of symmetry, the two halves would be mirror images of each other. Suppose (a, b) is in quadrant I. Then $(-a, b)$ would be in quadrant II, $(-a, -b)$ would be in quadrant III, and $(a, -b)$ would be in quadrant IV, as shown.

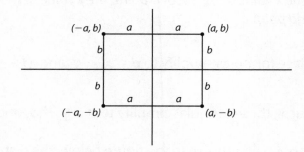

LINE SEGMENTS

Distance and Midpoint

The formulas for distance and midpoint look a little complicated, but they are fairly easy to use. It just takes practice.

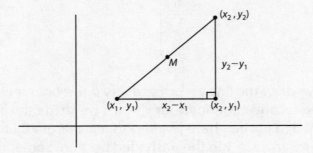

To find the **distance** between two points (x_1, y_1) and (x_2, y_2) on a plane, we must use the distance formula:

$$d = \sqrt{(x_2 - x_1)^2 + (y_2 - y_1)^2}$$

The distance formula is just the Pythagorean Theorem (discussed later in this chapter).

Distances are always positive. You may be six feet tall, but you cannot be minus six feet tall.

The **midpoint** of a line between two points (x_1, y_1) and (x_2, y_2) on a plane is given by

$$M = \left(\frac{x_1 + x_2}{2}, \frac{y_1 + y_2}{2} \right)$$

Note *In the notation x_1 the "1" is a subscript. It means the x value of the first point. Similarly x_2, y_1, and y_2 are the x value of the second point, the y value of the first point, and the y value of the second point.*

If the line is horizontal, these formulas simplify to $d = x_2 - x_1$ and $M = \frac{x_1 + x_2}{2}$

Similarly, if the line is vertical, these formulas simplify to $d = y_2 - y_1$ and $M = \frac{y_1 + y_2}{2}$

For example, for the horizontal line shown in the figure below, the distance between the points is $d = x_2 - x_1 = 7 - (-3) = 10$, and the midpoint is $M = \frac{x_1 + x_2}{2} = \frac{-3 + 7}{2} = 2$.

Similarly, for the vertical line shown in the figure below, the distance between the points is $d = y_2 - y_1 = -3 - (-7) = 4$, and the midpoint is $M = \dfrac{y_1 + y_2}{2} = \dfrac{(-7) + (-3)}{2} = -5$.

Example 1:   Find the distance between the points and the midpoint of the line segment joining these points:

    a. $(2, 3)$ and $(6, 8)$
    b. $(4, -3)$ and $(-2, 0)$
    c. $(7, 3)$ and $(4, 3)$
    d. $(2, 1)$ and $(2, 5)$

Solutions:

    a. We let $(x_1, y_1) = (2, 3)$ and $(x_2, y_2) = (6, 8)$, although the other way around is also okay.

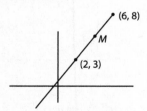

Then

Distance =
$$d = \sqrt{(x_2 - x_1)^2 + (y_2 - y_1)^2} = \sqrt{(6 - 2)^2 + (8 - 3)^2} = \sqrt{41} \approx 6.4$$
(by calculator)

$$\text{Midpoint} = M = \left(\frac{x_1 + x_2}{2}, \frac{y_1 + y_2}{2} \right) = \left(\frac{2 + 6}{2}, \frac{3 + 8}{2} \right) = (4, 5.5)$$

b. We let $(x_1, y_1) = (4, -3) =$ and $(x_2, y_2) = (-2, 0)$.

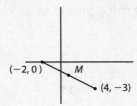

Distance $= d = \sqrt{(-2 - 4)^2 + (0 - (-3))^2} = \sqrt{45} = \sqrt{3 \times 3 \times 5} = 3\sqrt{5} \approx 6.7$

Midpoint $= M = \left(\dfrac{4 + (-2)}{2}, \dfrac{-3 + 0}{2} \right) = (1, -1.5)$

c. We let $(x_1, y_1) = (7, 3) =$ and $(x_2, y_2) = (4, 3)$.

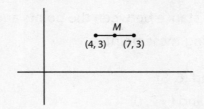

It is a one-dimensional distance, so $d = |4 - 7| = 3$

Midpoint $= M = \left(\dfrac{7 + 4}{2}, \dfrac{3 + 3}{2} \right) = (5.5, 3)$

d. We let $(x_1, y_1) = (2, 1) =$ and $(x_2, y_2) = (2, 5)$.

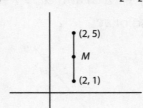

Again, this is a one-dimensional distance, so $d = |5 - 1| = 4$

Midpoint $= M = \left(\dfrac{2 + 2}{2}, \dfrac{5 + 1}{2} \right) = (2, 3)$

Example 2:   Find the distance and midpoint between the following points:

a. (1, 5) and (7, 3)
b. (−2, 5) and (7, −8)
c. (4, 3) and (−2, 3)
d. (1, 7) and (1, 4)

Solutions

a. Let (x_1, y_1) be $(1, 5)$ (could have been the other point), so $x_1 = 1$ and $y_1 = 5$. Let (x_2, y_2) be $(7, 3)$, so $x_2 = 7$ and $y_2 = 3$. Then the distance between the points is

$$d = \sqrt{(x_2 - x_1)^2 + (y_2 - y_1)^2} = \sqrt{(7 - 1)^2 + (3 - 5)^2} = \sqrt{6^2 + (-2)^2} = \sqrt{40} \approx 6.3$$

The midpoint between the two points is

$$M = \left(\frac{x_1 + x_2}{2}, \frac{y_1 + y_2}{2} \right) = \left(\frac{1 + 7}{2}, \frac{3 + 5}{2} \right) = (4, 4)$$

b. $d = \sqrt{(7 - (-2))^2 + (-8 - (5))^2} = \sqrt{81 + 169} = \sqrt{250} \approx 15.8$ and

$$M = \left(\frac{7 + (-2)}{2}, \frac{-8 + 5}{2} \right) = (2.5, -1.5)$$

c. $d = \sqrt{(-2 - 4)^2 + (3 - 3)^2} = \sqrt{36} = 6$ and $M = \left(\frac{-2 + 4}{2}, \frac{3 + 3}{2} \right) = (1, 3)$

d. $d = \sqrt{(1 - 1)^2 + (4 - 7)^2} = \sqrt{9} = 3$ and $M = \left(\frac{1 + 1}{2}, \frac{4 + 7}{2} \right) = (1, 5.5)$

Before I wrote the next part of this chapter, I formulated in my head how it would go. Too many of the questions on angles had to do with triangles. So I decided to write them together.

TYPES OF ANGLES

There are several ways to classify angles, such as by angle measure, as shown here:

Acute angle: An angle of less than 90°.

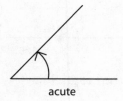

acute

Right angle: A 90° angle. As we will see, some other words that indicate a right angle are *perpendicular (⊥)*, *altitude*, and *height*.

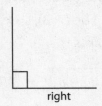

right

Obtuse angle: An angle of more than 90° but less than 180°.

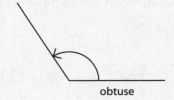

obtuse

Straight angle: An angle of 180°.

straight

Reflex angle: An angle of more than 180° but less than 360°.

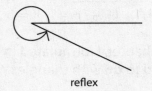

reflex

Angles are also named for their relation to other angles, such as:

Supplementary angles: Two angles that total 180°.

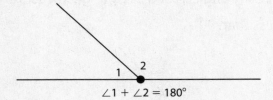

$\angle 1 + \angle 2 = 180°$

Complementary angles: Two angles that total 90°.

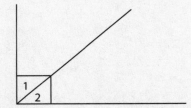

A Note of Interest: Once around a circle is 360°. The reason that it is 360° is that the ancient Babylonians, about 7000 years ago, thought there were 360 days in a year. Three hundred sixty degrees is unique to the planet Earth.

ANGLES FORMED BY PARALLEL LINES

Let's look at angles formed when a line crosses two parallel lines. Parallel lines are lines that never intersect; they are always the same distance apart. In the figure below, $\ell_1 \parallel \ell_2$, and t is a **transversal**, a line that cuts two or more lines.

It is not important that you know the names of these angles, although many of you will. It is important only to know that angles formed by a line crossing parallel lines that look equal are equal. The angles that are not equal add to 180°. In this figure, $\angle 1 = \angle 4 = \angle 5 = \angle 8$ and $\angle 2 = \angle 3 = \angle 6 = \angle 7$. Any angle from the first group added to any angle from the second group totals 180°.

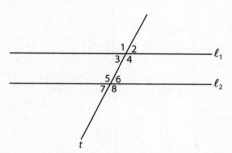

Vertical angles, which are the opposite angles formed when two lines cross, are equal. In the figure below, $\angle 1 = \angle 3$ and $\angle 2 = \angle 4$. Also, $\angle 1 + \angle 2 = \angle 2 + \angle 3 = \angle 3 + \angle 4 = \angle 4 + \angle 1$ 180°.

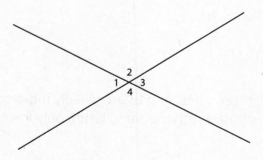

Example 3:

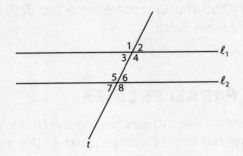

In the figure, $\ell_1 \parallel \ell_2$. If $\angle 3 = 65°$, find all the other angles.

Solution: $\angle 2 = \angle 6 = \angle 7 = 65°$ and $\angle 1 = \angle 4 = \angle 5 = \angle 8 = 180° - 65° = 115°$.

Example 4:

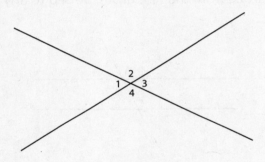

In the figure, If $\angle 2 = 98°$, find the other angles.

Solution: $\angle 4 = 98°$ and $\angle 1 = \angle 3 = 180° - 98° = 82°$

TRIANGLES

Basics about Triangles

A **triangle** is a polygon with three sides. Angles are usually indicated with capital letters. The side opposite the angle is indicated with the same letter, only lowercase.

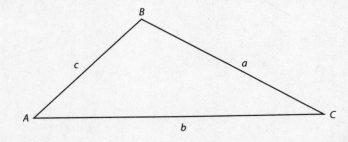

You should know the following general facts about triangles.

The **sum of the angles** of a triangle is 180°.

The **altitude**, or **height** (h), of $\triangle ABC$ shown below is the line segment drawn from a vertex perpendicular to the base, extended if necessary. The **base** of the triangle is $AC = b$.

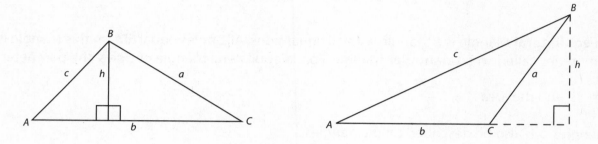

The **perimeter of a triangle** is the sum of the three sides: $p = a + b + c$.

The **area of a triangle** is $A = \frac{1}{2}bh$. The reason is that a triangle is half a rectangle. Because the area of a rectangle is base time height; a triangle is half a rectangle, as shown in the figure below.

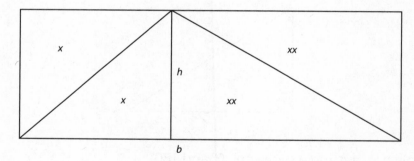

There are many kinds of triangles. One way to describe them is by their sides.

A **scalene** triangle has three unequal sides and three unequal angles.

An **isosceles** triangle has at least two equal sides. In the figure below, side BC (or a) is called the **base**; it may be equal to, greater than, or less than any other side. The **legs**, $AB = AC$ (or $b = c$) are equal. Angle A is the **vertex angle**; it may equal the others, or be greater than or less than the others. The **base angles** are equal: $\angle B = \angle C$.

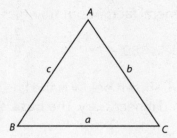

An **equilateral** triangle is a triangle with all equal sides. All angles equal 60°, so this triangle is sometimes called an **equiangular** triangle. For an equilateral triangle of side *s*, the perimeter $p = 3s$, and the area $A = \frac{s^2\sqrt{3}}{4}$.

Triangles can also be described by their angles.

An **acute** triangle has three angles that are less than 90°.

A **right triangle** has one right angle, as shown in the figure below. The **right angle** is usually denoted by the capital letter *C*. The **hypotenuse** *AB* is the side opposite the right angle. The **legs**, *AC* and *BC*, are not necessarily equal. $\angle A$ and $\angle B$ are always **acute** angles.

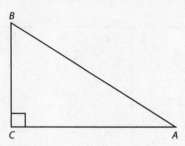

An **obtuse** triangle has one angle between 90° and 180°.

An **exterior angle** of a triangle is formed by extending one side. In the figure below, $\angle 1$ is an exterior angle. An exterior angle equals the sum of its two remote interior angles: $\angle 1 = \angle A + \angle B$.

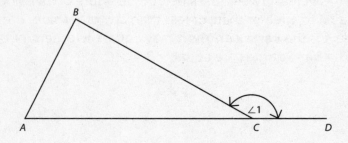

There are two other facts about triangles you should know:

1. The sum of any two sides of a triangle must be greater than the third side.

2. The largest side lies opposite the largest angle; and the largest angle lies opposite the largest side, as shown in the figure below.

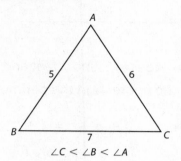

$$\angle C < \angle B < \angle A$$

Example 5:　Give one set of angles for a triangle that satisfies the following descriptions. (The solutions shown here are not the only correct answers. All angles must total 180°.)

Descriptions	Solutions
a. Scalene, acute	50°, 60°, 70° (no angle can be 90° or more; no two angles can be equal)
b. Scalene, right	30°, 60°, 90° (one angle must be 90°; the other two angles cannot be equal)
c. Scalene, obtuse	30°, 50°, 100° (one angle must be greater than 90°; the other two angles cannot be equal)
d. Isosceles, acute	20°, 80°, 80° (no angle can be 90° or more; two angles must be equal)
e. Isosceles, right	45°, 45°, 90° (this is the only answer)
f. Isosceles, obtuse	20°, 20°, 140° (one angle must be greater than 90°; the other two angles must be equal)
g. Equilateral	60°, 60°, 60° (this is the only answer)

Let's next look at some more examples with angles. Then we'll turn to area and perimeter exercises. We'll finish the chapter with our old friend Pythagoras and his famous theorem.

Example 6:

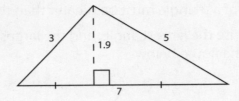

A triangle has sides 3, 5, and 7 feet and a height to the base of 1.9 feet, as shown in the figure. Find the perimeter and area of the triangle.

Solution: The perimeter $p = a + b + c = 3 + 7 + 5 = 15$ feet. The area $A = \frac{1}{2}bh = \frac{1}{2}(7)(1.9) = 6.65$ square feet.

Example 7:

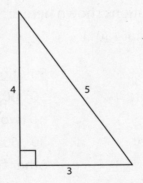

A right triangle with dimensions 3, 4, and 5 meters is shown. Find the perimeter and the area of the triangle.

Solution: $p = a + b + c = 3 + 4 + 5 = 12$ meters. Because the legs form a 90° angle, as indicated by the box in the corner, one leg can be the base and the other the height. $A = \frac{1}{2}bh = \frac{1}{2}(4)(3) = 6$ square meters, which can be also written 6 m².

Example 8:

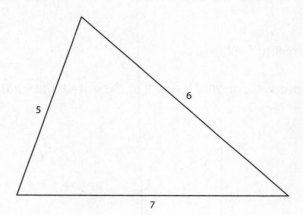

The triangle shown has sides 5, 6, and 7 yards. Find the perimeter and area.

Solution: $p = 5 + 6 + 7 = 18$ yards. To find the area, you need to find the height, which involves more math than is required for the TABE.

Example 9:   The area of a triangle is 100 square feet. If the base is 10 feet, find the height.

Solution: $A = \frac{1}{2}bh$. Substitute the known values to get $100 = \frac{1}{2}(10)(h)$. So $5h = 100$, and $h = 20$ feet.

Example 10:   Given the following two angles of a triangle, find the missing angle and describe the triangle in two ways, by its angles and by its sides.

Problems	Solutions
a. 40°, 30°	110°, obtuse and scalene
b. 65°, 50°	65°, acute and isosceles
c. 10°, 80°	90°, right and scalene
d. 60°, 60°	60°, equiangular and equilateral
e. 130°, 25°	25°, obtuse and isosceles

PYTHAGOREAN THEOREM

This is perhaps the most famous math theorem (a proven law) of all. Most theorems have one proof. A small fraction of these have two. This theorem, however, has more than a hundred, including three by past presidents of the United States. We've had some smart presidents who actually knew some math.

The Pythagorean Theorem simply states:

In a right triangle, the hypotenuse squared is equal to the sum of the squares of the legs.

In symbols, $c^2 = a^2 + b^2$.

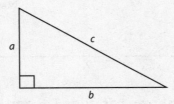

As a teacher, I must show you one proof.

Proof:

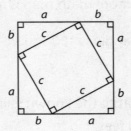

In this figure, the larger square equals the smaller square plus the four congruent triangles. In symbols, $(a + b)^2 = c^2 + 4\left(\frac{1}{2}ab\right)$.

Multiplying this equation out, we get $a^2 + 2ab + b^2 = c^2 + 2ab$. Then canceling $2ab$ from both sides, we get $c^2 = a^2 + b^2$. The proof is complete.

There are two basic problems the Pythagorean Theorem helps you to know how to do: finding the hypotenuse and finding one of the legs of the right triangle.

Example 11: Solve for *x*:

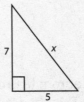

Solution: $x^2 = 7^2 + 5^2$; $x = \sqrt{74} \approx 8.6$.

Example 12: Solve for x:

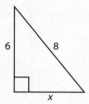

Solution: $8^2 = 6^2 + x^2$, or $x^2 = 64 - 36 = 28$. So $x = \sqrt{28} \approx 5.3$.

Notice that the hypotenuse squared is always by itself, whether it is a number or a letter.

Pythagorean Triples

Because no calculator is allowed on part of the exam, it is a good idea to memorize some Pythagorean triples. These are the sides of a triangle that are *always* right triangles. The hypotenuse is always listed third in the group.

The 3-4-5 group: 3-4-5, 6-8-10, 9-12-15, 12-16-20, 15-20-25

The 5-12-13 group: 5-12-13, 10-24-26

The rest: 8-15-17, 7-24-25, 20-21-29, 9-40-41, 11-60-61

Notes

1. For the TABE, it really is a good idea to memorize the 3-4-5 and 5-12-13 groups. Unless you like to memorize things or are a nerd like me, you don't have to memorize the others because they most likely will not be on the exam.

2. From the few exam types I've seen, the TABE seems to ask about only exact square roots. However, I'm not positive; so I'm including exact and inexact square roots. If the square root is not exact, it will never be on the part without a calculator.

> **Example 13:** A right triangle has leg 6 inches and leg 8 inches. Find the hypotenuse, the perimeter, and the area.

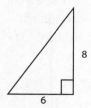

Solution: $x = \sqrt{6^2 + 8^2} = 10$ inches; $p = a + b + c = 6 + 8 + 10 = 24$ inches. $A = \dfrac{1}{2}bh = \dfrac{1}{2}(6)(8) = 24$ square inches, or 24 in². What is the significance that both answers are 24? Absolutely nothing!

Example 14: A right triangle has leg 12 timlocks and hypotenuse 13 timlocks. Find the other leg, the perimeter, and the area.

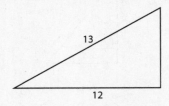

Solution:

$a^2 + b^2 = c^2$; $b^2 = c^2 - a^2 = 13^2 - 12^2 = 25$; so $b = 5$ timlocks (a made-up measurement, in case you were curious). So $b = 5$; $p = 5 + 12 + 13 = 30$ timlocks; $A = \dfrac{1}{2}(5)(12) = 30$ square timlocks.

Example 15: Find the perimeter and area of an equilateral triangle whose side is 10 kilometers (big!).

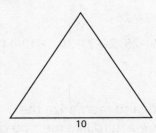

Solution:

$p = 10 + 10 + 10 = 30$ kilometers;

$A = \dfrac{s^2\sqrt{3}}{4} = \dfrac{10 \times 10 \times \sqrt{3}}{4} = 25\sqrt{3} \approx 43.3.$

The way I remember $\sqrt{3} \approx 1.732$ is that it was the year George Washington was born. This was told to me by my high school geometry teacher, Ms. Griswold, the best math teacher I ever had. I took a lot of math courses and, fortunately for me, I had a number of very good ones.

Notes

1. I have an aunt who lived at a house with a street number 1732. I cannot forget the house number. She has moved several times since then. I know none of the other ones.

2: Just in case you were wondering, $\sqrt{2} \approx 1.414$.

Ⓠ **Let's do some exercises.**

Calculators are permitted for these exercises.

Exercise 1: The figure formed by two rays with a common endpoint is called a(n)

     A. Line   **C.** Angle

     B. Line segment   **D.** Triangle

Exercise 2: In a triangle, a line segment at a 90° angle with the base from a vertex is

     A. Perpendicular to the base

     B. An altitude

     C. A height

     D. All three of these

Exercise 3: The sum of the angles of a triangle is

     A. 90°   **C.** 360°

     B. 180°   **D.** 720°

Exercise 4: An angle that is more than 90° but less than 180° is

     A. Acute   **C.** Obtuse

     B. Right   **D.** Straight

Exercise 5: Two angles of a triangle are 40° and 70°. The triangle is

     A. Right and scalene   **C.** Right and isosceles

     B. Acute and scalene   **D.** Acute and isosceles

Exercise 6:   Two angles of a triangle are 25° and 45°. The triangle is

A. Acute and scalene   C. Obtuse and scalene

B. Acute and isosceles   D. Obtuse and isosceles

Exercise 7:   Two angles that add to 180° are

A. Equal   C. Complementary

B. Vertical   D. Supplementary

Exercise 8:   Vertical angles are

A. Equal   C. Supplementary

B. Complementary   D. Add to 360°

Exercise 9:   The largest side of a right triangle is the

A. Altitude   C. Leg

B. Median   D. Hypotenuse

Exercise 10: A line segment drawn from a vertex to the middle of the opposite side is a(n)

A. Altitude   C. Median

B. Bisector   D. Diameter

Exercise 11: Let N (−3, −2) and P (5, 4) be two points. The midpoint of NP is

A. (4, 3)   C. (−4, −3)

B. (1, 1)   D. 0

Exercise 12: Let N (−3, −2) and P (5, 4) be two points. The length of NP is

A. 10   C. 14

B. 12   D. 16

Exercise 13: In a triangle, the angle ratio is 2 to 3 to 5. The smallest angle is

A. 18°   C. 54°

B. 36°   D. 90°

Exercise 14:   A triangle has base 12, and height to that base is 8. Its area is

      A. 48   **C.** 72

      B. 64   **D.** 96

Exercise 15:   A right triangle of sides 5, 12, 13 has area

      A. 30   **C.** 48

      B. 42   **D.** 60

Exercise 16:   The perimeter of the triangle in Exercise 15 is

      A. 30   **C.** 48

      B. 42   **D.** 60

Exercise 17:   The perimeter of an equilateral triangle of side 12 is

      A. 18   **C.** 54

      B. 36   **D.** $36\sqrt{3}$

Exercise 18:   If the hypotenuse is 15 and one leg is 9, the other leg is

      A. 12   **C.** 18

      B. 15   **D.** 24

Exercise 19:   If two sides of a triangle are 6 and 9, the third side cannot be

      A. 13   **C.** 6

      B. 9   **D.** 2

Exercise 20:   In triangle *ABC*, *AB* = 5, *BC* = 6, and *AC* = 7. The largest angle is

      A. A   **C.** C

      B. B   **D.** Can't tell

Let's look at the answers

Answer 1:   C: This is the definition of an angle.

Answer 2:   D

Answer 3:   B

Answer 4:   C

Answer 5:   D: The third angle is $180° - 40° - 70° = 70°$; all angles are less than $90°$ (acute) and two angles are equal (isosceles).

Answer 6:   C: The third angle is $110°$ (obtuse); all angles are unequal (scalene).

Answer 7:   D

Answer 8:   A

Answer 9:   D

Answer 10:   C

Answer 11:   B: $\left(\dfrac{-3+5}{2}, \dfrac{-2+4}{2}\right)$

Answer 12:   A: $\sqrt{(-3-5)^2 + (-2-4)^2} = \sqrt{(-8)^2 + (-6)^2} = \sqrt{100} = 10.$

Answer 13:   B: $2x + 3x + 5x = 180$; $10x = 180°$; $x = 18°$; The smallest angle is $2x = 2(18) = 36°.$

Answer 14:   A: $A = \dfrac{1}{2}(12)(8) = 48.$

Answer 15:   A: Drawing the picture, we see the base and height are 12 and 5 (one is the base and the other is the height); $A = \dfrac{1}{2}(12)(5) = 30.$

Answer 16:   A: In this case, the perimeter is also $30 = 5 + 12 + 13$.

Answer 17:   B: $12 + 12 + 12 = 36$.

Answer 18:   A: $\sqrt{15^2 - 9^2} = \sqrt{144} = 12$

Answer 19:   D: The third side x must be between $9 - 6 < x < 9 + 6$.

Answer 20:   B: It is the angle opposite AC, the longest side.

Let's do more geometry.

"*Mastering all shapes and sizes will enhance your journey. We now deal with the rest of the polygons (closed figures with line-segment sides).*"

QUADRILATERALS

Parallelograms

A **parallelogram** is a quadrilateral (four-sided polygon) with parallel opposite sides.

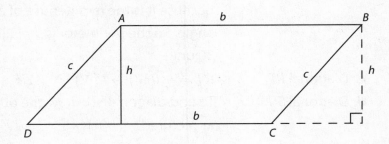

You should know the following properties about parallelograms:

- The opposite angles are equal. $\angle DAB = \angle BCD$ and $\angle ADC = \angle ABC$.

- The consecutive angles are supplementary. $\angle DAB + \angle ABC = \angle ABC + \angle BCD = \angle BCD + \angle CDA = \angle CDA + \angle DAB = 180°$.

- The opposite sides are equal. $AB = CD$ and $AD = BC$.

- The diagonals bisect each other. $AE = EC$ and $DE = EB$.

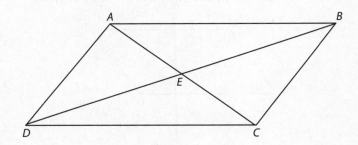

- Area $= A = bh$. This is a postulate (law taken to be true without proof) from which we get the area of all other figures with sides that are line segments.

- Perimeter $= p = 2b + 2c$.

Example 1:   For parallelogram *RSTU*, find the following if *RU* = 10:

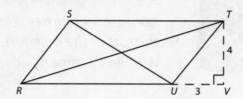

Problems	Solutions
<u>Problems</u>	<u>Solutions</u>
a. The area	$A = bh = (10)(4) = 40$ square units. The whole test should be this easy!
b. The perimeter	We have to find the length of $RS = TU$. $TU = 5$ because it is the hypotenuse of a 3-4-5 right triangle. So the perimeter is $p = 2(10) + 2(5) = 30$ units.
c. Diagonal *RT*	$RT = \sqrt{(RV)^2 + (TV)^2} = \sqrt{13^2 + 4^2} = \sqrt{185}$
d. Diagonal *SU*	To find diagonal SU, draw the other altitude SW as pictured.

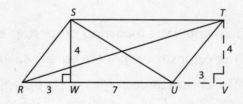

$$SU = \sqrt{WU^2 + SW^2} = \sqrt{7^2 + 4^2} = \sqrt{65}$$

Example 2:   For parallelogram *EFGH*, find the smaller angle.

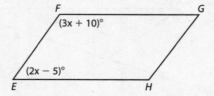

Solution: Consecutive angles of a parallelogram are supplementary. Therefore, $(3x + 10)° + (2x - 5)° = 180°$; $x = 35°$; so the smaller angle is $2(35°) - 5° = 65°$. Be careful to give the answer the TABE wants. Two of the other choices would be 35° and 115°, for those who do not read carefully!!!

Rhombus

A **rhombus** is an equilateral parallelogram.

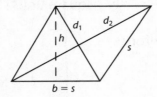

Thus, a rhombus has all of the properties of a parallelogram plus the following:

- All sides s are equal.
- The diagonals are perpendicular to each other.
- Perimeter $= p = 4s$.
- Area $= A = bh = \frac{1}{2} \times d_1 \times d_2$, or, the area equals half the product of its diagonals.

Example 3:   For the given rhombus with side $s = 13$ and larger diagonal $BD = 24$, find the other diagonal and the area.

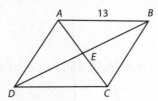

Solutions: $AB = 13$ and $BD = 24$. Because the diagonals bisect each other, $BE = 12$. The diagonals are perpendicular to each other, so $\triangle ABE$ is a 5-12-13 right triangle, and $AE = 5$. Therefore, the other diagonal $AC = 10$. The area $A = \frac{1}{2} \times d_1 \times d_2 = \frac{1}{2}(24)(10) = 120$ square units.

Example 4: Find the area of a rhombus with side 10 and smaller interior angle of 60°.

Solution: If you draw the diagonal through the two larger angles, you will have two congruent equilateral triangles. The area of this rhombus is twice the area of each triangle, or $2 \times \dfrac{s^2\sqrt{3}}{4}$. Because $s = 10$, the area is

$$A = 2 \times \frac{10^2\sqrt{3}}{4} = 50\sqrt{3} \text{ square units.}$$

Now let's go on to more familiar territory.

Rectangle

A **rectangle** is a parallelogram with right angles. Therefore, it has all of the properties of a parallelogram plus the following:

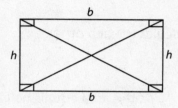

- All angles are 90°.
- Diagonals are equal (but *not* perpendicular).
- Perimeter = $p = 2b + 2h$
- Area = $A = bh$

The easier the shape, the more likely the TABE will have a problem or problems about it.

Example 5: In a rectangle, one base is 8 and one diagonal is 9. Find all the sides and the other diagonal. Find the perimeter and area.

Solution: The top base and bottom base are both 8. Both diagonals are 9. The other two sides are each $\sqrt{9^2 - 8^2} = \sqrt{17} \approx 4.1$. So the perimeter is $p = 16 + 2\sqrt{17} \approx 24.2$ units; and the area is $A = 8\sqrt{17} \approx 32.98$ square units.

Example 6: $AB = 10$, $BC = 8$, $EF = 6$, and $FG = 3$. Find the area of the shaded region of the figure.

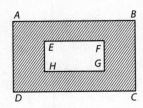

Solution: The area of the shaded region is the area of the outside rectangle minus the area of the inside one. $A = (10)(8) - (6)(3) = 62$ square units.

Example 7:   In polygon $ABCDEF$, $BC = 30$, $AF = 18$, $AB = 20$, and $CD = 11$. Find the perimeter and area of the polygon.

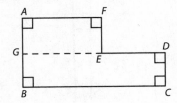

Solution: Draw a line through DE, hitting AB at point G. Then $AF = GE$ and $BC = GD$. Because $DG = 30$ and $GE = 18$, $DE = 12$. $AB = CD + EF$. $AB = 20$ and $CD = 11$, so $EF = 9$. This gives the lengths of all the sides. The perimeter thus is $p = AB + BC + CD + DE + EF + AF = 30 + 20 + 11 + 12 + 9 + 18 = 100$ units.

The area of rectangle $BCDG$ is $BC \times CD = (30)(11) = 330$. The area of rectangle $AFEG$ is $AF \times FE = (18)(9) = 162$. Therefore, the total area is $330 + 162 = 492$ square units. There are other ways to find this area, as you might be able to see.

Square

A **square** is a rectangle with equal sides, or it can be thought of as a rhombus with four equal 90° angles. Therefore, it has all of the properties of a rectangle and a rhombus:

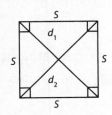

- All sides are equal.
- All angles are 90°.
- Both diagonals bisect each other, are perpendicular to each other, and are equal.
- Each diagonal $d = d_1 = d_2 = s\sqrt{2}$, where s = a side.
- Perimeter $= p = 4s$
- Area $= A = \dfrac{d^2}{2} = s^2$

There are odd shapes that the TABE sometimes mentions. One is the **kite**, with the following properties:

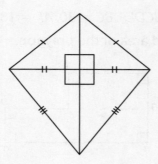

- It has two pairs of equal sides.
- The diagonals are perpendicular.
- One diagonal is bisected.

Another shape is the **arrowhead**, with the following properties:

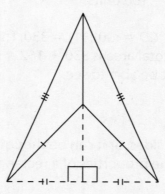

- It has two pairs of equal sides.
- If the diagonals are extended, they meet at right angles (they are perpendicular).
- If the diagonal through the angles between the equal sides is extended, it bisects the other diagonal.

Let's do a few problems on the basic shapes.

Example 8:   Find the area, perimeter, and diagonal of a square with side 8.

Solution: $A = 8^2 = 64$ square units; $p = 4s = 4(8) = 32$ units; $d = 8\sqrt{2} \approx 11.3$ units

Example 9:

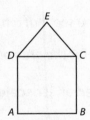

Find the area of this square.

Solution: A square has equal sides; so $5x - 1 = x + 1$; $4x = 2$; $x = \dfrac{1}{2}$. Then each of

$5x - 1$ and $x + 1$ is $\dfrac{3}{2}$. $A = s^2 = \left(\dfrac{3}{2}\right)\left(\dfrac{3}{2}\right) = \dfrac{9}{4}$ square units.

Example 10:

This figure is a square surmounted by an equilateral triangle. (I've always wanted to write that word.) $CE = 10$. What are the perimeter and area of the figure?

Solution: The perimeter is $p = 5(10) = 50$. Note that CD is *not* part of the perimeter, but all of the other line segments are equal.

The area is the area of the square plus the area of the triangle:

$$A = s^2 + \frac{s^2\sqrt{3}}{4} = 10^2 + \frac{10^2\sqrt{3}}{4} = 25(4 + \sqrt{3}).$$

TRAPEZOID

A **trapezoid** is a quadrilateral with exactly one pair of parallel sides.

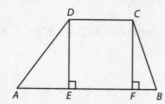

Because a trapezoid is *not* a type of parallelogram, it has its own unique set of properties, as follows:

- The parallel sides, *AB* and *CD*, are called **bases**.
- The heights, *DE* and *CF*, are equal.
- The legs, *AD* and *BC*, may or may not be equal.
- The diagonals, *AC* and *BD*, may or may not be equal.
- Perimeter = $p = AB + BC + CD + AD$.

- Area = $A = \frac{1}{2}h(b_1 + b_2)$, where b_1 and b_2 are the bases.

Note *If we draw one of the diagonals, we see that a trapezoid is the sum of two triangles. Factoring out $\frac{1}{2}h$, we get the formula for the area of the trapezoid.*

If the legs are equal, the trapezoid is called an **isosceles trapezoid**, shown below.

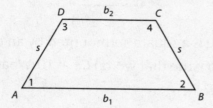

An isosceles trapezoid has the additional properties:

- Perimeter = $p = b_1 + b_2 + 2s$.
- The diagonals are equal, $AC = BD$.
- The base angles are equal, $\angle 1 = \angle 2$ and $\angle 3 = \angle 4$.

Example 11:

Find the perimeter and area of Figure *ABCD*.

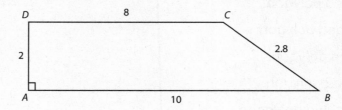

Solution: The perimeter is $p = 10 + 2 + 8 + 2.8 = 22.8$, and the area is
$A = \frac{1}{2}h(b_1 + b_2) = \frac{1}{2}(2)(8 + 10) = 18$.

Example 12: Find the area of isosceles trapezoid *EFGH*.

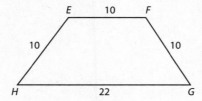

Solution: Draw in the two heights for the trapezoid.

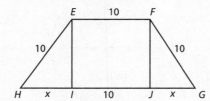

The two bases of the triangles formed are equal because it is an isosceles trapezoid. From the figure, $2x + 10 = 22$, so $x = 6$. Each of the triangles is a 6-8-10 Pythagorean triple, so the

height of the trapezoid is 8. Therefore, $A = \frac{1}{2}(8)(10 + 22) = 128$.

POLYGONS

Let's talk about polygons in general. Most of the time we deal with **regular polygons**. A regular polygon has all sides equal and all angles equal. A square and an equilateral triangle are examples of regular polygons we have already discussed.

Polygons are named for the number of sides they have. For the TABE, we need to know the names of these figures:

A **pentagon** is a 5-sided polygon.

A **hexagon** is a 6-sided polygon.

A **heptagon** is a 7-sided polygon.

An **octagon** is an 8-sided polygon.

A **nonagon** is a 9-sided polygon.

A **decagon** is a 10-sided polygon.

A **dodecagon** is a 12-sided polygon.

An **n-gon** is an *n*-sided polygon.

We now need to take a look at circles.

CIRCLES

Parts of a Circle

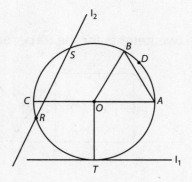

We all know what a circle looks like, but maybe we're not familiar with its "parts."

O is the **center** of the circle. A circle is often named by its center, so this is circle *O*.

OA, OT, OC, and *OB* are **radii** (singular: radius); a radius is a line segment from the center to the **circumference**, or edge, of the circle.

Note *All radii (r) of a circle are equal. This is a postulate or axiom, a law taken to be true without proof. It is probably a good idea to tell you there are no proofs on the TABE, as there are in a geometry course.*

AC is the **diameter**, *d*, the distance from one side of the circle through the center to the other side; $d = 2r$, and $r = \dfrac{d}{2}$.

ℓ_1 is a **tangent**, a line that touches a circle in one and only one point.

T is a **point of tangency**, the point where a tangent touches the circle. The radius to the point of tangency (*OT*) is always perpendicular to the tangent, so $OT \perp \ell_1$.

ℓ_2 is a **secant**, a line that passes through a circle in two places.

RS is a **chord**, a line segment that has each end on the circumference of the circle. The **diameter** is the longest chord in a circle.

OADBO is a **sector** (a pie-shaped part of a circle). There are a number of sectors in this figure; others include *BOCSB* and *OATRCSBO*. We will see these again soon.

An **arc** is any distance along the circumference of a circle.

Arc *ADB* is a **minor arc** because it is less than half a circle.

Arc *BDATRC* is a **major arc** because it is more than half a circle.

Arc *ATRC* is a **semicircle** because it is exactly half a circle.

Whew! Enough! However, we do need some more facts about circles.

The following are mostly theorems, proven laws. Again, there are no proofs on the TABE, but you need to be aware of these facts.

Area and Circumference

Area of a circle:

$$A = \pi r^2$$

Circumference (perimeter of a circle):

$$C = 2\pi r \text{ or } \pi d.$$

On this test, π is approximately 3.14 or, less accurately, $\dfrac{22}{7}$.

Example 13:   Find the circumference and area of a circle of diameter 140. Use the approximation $\frac{22}{7}$ for π.

Solution: If $d = 140$, then $r = 70$. $C = 2\pi r = 2\left(\frac{22}{7}\right)(70) = 440$ units. $A = \pi r^2 = \left(\frac{22}{7}\right)(70)(70) = 15{,}400$ square units.

Sectors

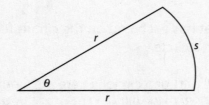

Area of a sector:

$$A = \frac{\theta}{360°}\pi r^2$$

where θ (theta) is the angle of the sector in degrees.

Arc length of a sector:

$$s = \frac{\theta}{360°}2\pi r,$$

Perimeter of a sector:

$$p = s + 2r,$$

where s is the arc length

Example 14:   Find the area and perimeter of a 60° sector of a circle of diameter 12.

Solution:

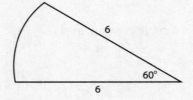

If the diameter is 12, the radius is 6. The sector is pictured here. Its area is $A = \dfrac{60^\circ}{360^\circ} \times \pi 6^2 = 6\pi$

square units. The perimeter of the sector is $s = 2(6) + \dfrac{60^\circ}{360^\circ} \times 2\pi(6) = 12 + 12\pi$ units.

Example 15:

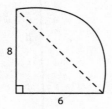

Find the perimeter and the area of this figure, which is half a circle on top of a right triangle.

Solution: The perimeter consists of the two legs of the right triangle and half a circle, a semicircle. Even though the dotted line is not part of the perimeter, we must find it because it is the diameter of the circle. If you see that this is again a 6–8–10 right triangle, the diameter of the semicircle is 10, so the radius is 5. The perimeter is

$$p = 6 + 8 + \left(\frac{1}{2}\right)(2\pi r) = 14 + 5\pi \approx 29.70 \text{ units. The area}$$

$$A = \left(\frac{1}{2}\right)bh + \left(\frac{1}{2}\right)\pi r^2 = \left(\frac{1}{2}\right)(6)(8) + \left(\frac{1}{2}\right)(3.14)(25) \approx 63.25 \text{ square}$$

units.

If you can do this problem, even after reading the solution, nothing in the geometric sections should bother you!

Example 16:

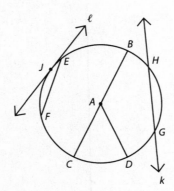

From this picture, identify all of the following by letters; there may be more than one answer.

Problems	Solutions
Radius	AB, AC, AD
Diameter	BC
Chord	EF, BC, GH
Tangent	ℓ
Secant line	k
Point of tangency	J

Example 17: For the figure in Example 16, if $AD = 10$ inches, find the circumference $C = \pi d$ and area $A = \pi r^2$, if $\pi = 3.14$.

Solution: Because $r = 10$, $d = 20$; $C = 20(3.14) = 62.8$ inches. $A = 3.14\,(10)\,(10) = 314$ square inches.

Note *Geometry has a lot of new vocabulary you must learn.*

A little history: 700 years ago, in the Dark Ages, the only math that educated people learned was geometry. They didn't learn it for calculus. Calculus hadn't been invented yet! They didn't learn it for algebra. Believe it or not, algebra wasn't in high school until after 1900. People learned geometry, mostly geometric proofs, to help in learning history, English, and philosophy! The logic you learn in doing geometric proofs is the same skill you need to write logical essays in English and history classes. Let's go on.

THREE-DIMENSIONAL FIGURES

There are five three-dimensional (3D) shapes you need to know about. I've also included two surface areas: one because of its significance and a second because I have a good story to tell about it.

Box

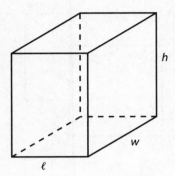

This figure is also known as a **rectangular solid**, and if that isn't a mouthful enough, its correct name is a **rectangular parallelepiped**. But essentially, it's a **box**.

- Volume = $V = \ell wh$

- Surface area = $SA = 2\ell w + 2\ell h + 2wh$

Example 18:   For the given figure, find V and SA.

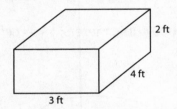

Solution: $V = \ell wh = (3)(4)(2) = 24$ cubic feet; $SA = 2\ell w + 2\ell h + 2wh = 2(3)(4) + 2(3)(2) + 2(4)(2) = 52$ square feet.

Cube

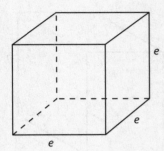

A **cube** is a box for which all of the faces, or sides, are equal squares.

- $V = e^3$ (read as "e cubed"). Cubing, which we discussed in an earlier chapter, comes from a cube!

- $SA = 6e^2$

- A cube has 6 faces, 8 vertices (corners), and 12 edges.

   Example 19: For a cube with an edge of 10 meters, find V and SA.

   Solution: $V = 10^3 = 1,000$ cubic meters; $SA = 6e^2 = 6(10)^2 = 600$ square meters.

Cylinder

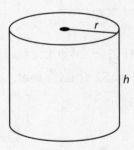

A **cylinder** is shaped like a can. The curved surface is considered as a side, and the top and bottom are equal circles.

- $V = \pi r^2 h$

- $SA = $ Area of (top + bottom + curved surface) $= 2\pi r^2 + 2\pi rh$

Once a neighbor of mine wanted to find the area of the curved part of a cylinder. He wasn't interested in why; just the answer. Of course, being a teacher, I had to explain it to him. I told him that if you cut a label off a soup can and unwrap it, the figure is a rectangle; neglecting the rim, the height is the height of the can and the width is the circumference of the circle. Multiply this height and width, and the answer is $2\pi r \times h$. He waited patiently and then soon moved. Just kidding!

In general, the volume of any figure for which the top is the same as the bottom is $V = Bh$,

where B is the area of the base. If the figure comes to a point, the volume is $\left(\dfrac{1}{3}\right) Bh$. The surface area is found by adding up all the sides.

Example 20: Find V and SA in terms of π for a cylinder of height 10 yards and diameter of 8 yards.

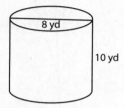

Solution: We see that, because $d = 8$, then $r = 4$. Then $V = \pi r^2 h = \pi(4^2 \times 10) = 160\pi$ cubic yards; $SA = 2\pi r^2 + 2\pi rh = 2\pi 4^2 + 2\pi(4)(10) = 112\pi$ square yards.

We need to know two more 3D figures.

Sphere

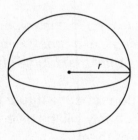

As many of you know, this is a **sphere**. Its volume is $V = \left(\dfrac{4}{3}\right) \pi r^3$, where r is the radius.

Example 21: Find the volume of a sphere if $r = 3$ and $\pi = 3.14$.

Solution: $V = \left(\dfrac{4}{3}\right) (3.14)(3)(3)(3) = 113.04$ cubic units.

Cone

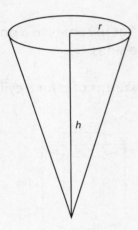

This is a **cone**. There is a story about this, too, but I'll skip it. The volume is $V = \left(\dfrac{1}{3}\right) \pi r^2 h$.

Example 22: Find the volume of a cone if $\pi = 3.14$, $r = 3$, and $h = 12$.

Solution: $V = \left(\dfrac{1}{3}\right)(3.14)(3)(3)(12) = 113.04$ cubic units. The answer is found by

calculator

Note *If the top of a 3D figure comes to a point, the volume is one-third the solid formed if the two bases are equal. So the volume of a cone is one-third the volume of a cylinder, and the volume of a pyramid is one-third the volume of a box.*

The TABE exam sometimes asks questions about a figure that you have never seen. If it involves a formula you don't know, it probably will be given to you. Otherwise, you may have to figure it out yourself. Let's look at one of them.

Example 23: Shown is a pyramid with a square base. $WX = 8$, $BV = 3$, and B is in the middle of the base.

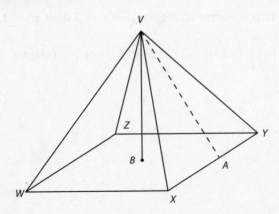

Find the volume, the surface area, and the length of *VY*.

Solution: The volume of this figure is $V = \left(\dfrac{1}{3}\right) s^2 h = \left(\dfrac{1}{3}\right)(8)^2(3) = 64$ cubic units.

The TABE would definitely give you this formula. (Notice the $\dfrac{1}{3}$ because the figure comes to a point.)

The surface area might be too difficult for the TABE, but let's do it because there are parts the TABE might ask about. There are five surfaces: one square base and four congruent triangles,

so the surface area is $SA = s^2 + 4\left(\dfrac{1}{2}bh\right)$. Now, because $s = WX = 8$, the triangle base $b = 8$.

We need to find the height of the triangle, *AV*, called the **slant height**. You must draw *AB*.

Because $XY = 8$, you need to see that $AB = \dfrac{1}{2}(8) = 4$. Triangle *ABV* is a right triangle (right

angle at *B*). It is also a 3–4–5 right triangle. So $AV = h = 5$. The surface area $SA = s^2 + 2bh = 8^2 + 2(8)(5) = 144$ square units.

If the TABE gave you the slant height, it might ask you to find *VY*. *VY* is the hypotenuse of triangle *VAY*, with the right angle at *A*. You should see that

$AY = \left(\dfrac{1}{2}\right)(8) = 4$, so $VY = \sqrt{4^2 + 5^2} = \sqrt{41} \approx 6.4$.

MEASUREMENTS

Now that we have all the shapes, let's talk about measuring them. In fact, let's talk about all the measurements we need.

Distances are measured two ways: the American system and the metric system.

American System

The standard measurements of length in the American system are:

12 **inches** = 1 **foot**

3 feet (or 36 inches) = 1 **yard**

5280 feet (or 1760 yards) = 1 **mile**

Example 24: Change 15 yards to feet.

Solution: There are two ways to look at this.

1. To go from a larger unit to a smaller unit, you multiply. To go from a smaller unit to a larger unit, you divide. Because feet are smaller than yards, and 3 feet = 1 yard, we multiply (15)(3) = 45 feet.

2. If you have trouble remembering the rule above, you can treat 3 feet = 1 yard as a fraction that equals 1 because they are equal.

We have 15 yards. We multiply 15 yards $\frac{3 \text{ feet}}{1 \text{ yard}}$. The yards cancel out and we get 45 feet.

If we want to convert 78 feet to yards, we get 78 feet $\frac{1 \text{ yard}}{3 \text{ feet}}$, and the feet now cancel out and we get 26 yards. We could just as well divide 78 by 3 because we are going from smaller to larger. You should use whichever way is better for you. Later, we'll show a longer problem to show the benefits of fractions.

Example 25:   Find the volume of a box that has length 3 feet, width 5 feet, and height 4 feet.

Solution: $V = \ell wh = 3(5)(4) = 60$ cubic feet.

Example 26:   Find the volume of a box that is 24 inches long by 10 feet wide by 3 yards high.

Solution: All the measurements must have the same units. Let's make them all feet: 24 inches ÷ 12 = 2 feet. 3 yards × (3) = 9 feet. then $V = \ell wh = 2(10)(9) = 180$ cubic feet.

Metric System

The standard measurements of length in the metric system are:

1,000 **millimeters** (mm) = 1 **meter** (m)

100 **centimeters** (cm) = 1 meter

1000 meters = 1 **kilometer** (km)

Example 27:   Change 4567 centimeters to meters, and change 23 kilometers to meters.

Solution: A centimeter is smaller than a meter, so divide: 4567 ÷ 100 = 45.67 meters. A kilometer is bigger than a meter, so multiply: 23 × 1,000 = 23,000 meters.

Note In the metric system, *milli* means $\frac{1}{1000}$, *centi* means $\frac{1}{100}$, and *kilo* means 1,000.

Example 28: A pool measures 50 meters by 45 meters.

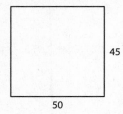

45

50

a. What is the perimeter?

b. What is the area of the pool?

c. If the pool is 2 meters deep, what is the volume?

d. If the pool can be filled at 600 cubic meters per hour, how long will it take to fill the pool?

Solutions:

a. The perimeter $p = 2\ell + 2w = 2(50) + 2(45) = 190$ meters

b. The area $A = bh$ or $\ell w = (50)(45) = 2{,}250$ square meters

c. The volume $V = \ell wh = (50)(45)2 = 4{,}500$ cubic meters

d. $\frac{4{,}500}{600} = 7.5$ hours to fill the pool

Note *There are 2.54 centimeters in one inch, 39.37 inches in a meter, and 1.61 kilometers in a mile.*

TIME

Most of you already know the basic units of time:

- 60 seconds in a minute
- 60 minutes in an hour
- 24 hours in a day
- 7 days in a week
- 365 (or 366 in leap year) days, or $52\frac{1}{7}$ (or $52\frac{2}{7}$) weeks, or 12 months in one year
- 10 years in a decade
- 10 decades or 100 years in a century

In sports and science, seconds are broken down further into tenths, hundredths, thousandths, and millionths of a second.

- A thousandth of a second is called a millisecond. Remember the prefix *milli* means $\frac{1}{1000}$.

- A millionth of a second is called a nanosecond. The prefix *nano* means $\frac{1}{1,000,000}$.

Example 29:

       a. How many years are in 223 decades?

       b. Two weeks is how many hours?

       c. How many nanoseconds in a millisecond?

Solutions:

       a. 223 decades × 10 = 2230 years

       b. $\frac{24 \text{ hours}}{1 \text{ day}} \times \frac{7 \text{ days}}{1 \text{ week}} \times 2 \text{ weeks} = 336$ hours in 2 weeks

       c. 1,000,000 nanoseconds are in a second, but 1000 milliseconds are in a second. So 1,000,000 ÷ 1000 = 1,000 nanoseconds in a millisecond.

LIQUID MEASURE

In the American system, the standard liquid measures are:

- 8 (liquid) **ounces** = 1 **pint**
- 2 pints = 1 **quart**
- 4 quarts = 1 **gallon**

In the metric system, the standard liquid measures are:

- 100 **centiliters** = 1 **liter**
- 10 **milliliters** = 1 centiliter

In case you were wondering, a 2-liter soda bottle is about 67.6 ounces.

Example 30:   One gallon of apple juice is on sale for $4.99. One quart of the same apple juice sells for $1.09. Which is a better price?

Solution: Four quarts (one gallon) of the $1.09 apple juice sells for $1.09 × 4 = $4.36, which is less than $4.99. The quart is a better price. On sale doesn't always mean cheaper!

Example 31:   Brand X ice cream sells for $2.50 a pint. Brand Y ice cream sells for $5.00 a half gallon. Which is a better buy?

Solution: There are 2 pints to the quart. There are 4 quarts in a gallon, and 4 pints in a half-gallon. Brand X costs 4 × $2.50 = $10.00 a half gallon, making Brand Y the better buy. However, you might like Brand X better, even though it's more expensive.

WEIGHT

In the American system, the standard measures of weight are:

- 16 **ounces** = 1 **pound** (these ounces are not the same as liquid ounces)
- 2,000 pounds = 1 **ton**

In the metric system, the standard measures of weight are:

- 1,000 **milligrams** (used for many drug measurements) = 1 **gram**
- 1,000 grams = 1 **kilogram** (used for Olympic weightlifters and the weight of Olympic athletes)

Again, in case you are wondering, there are 453 grams in a pound.

Example 32:   If a baby weighs 6 pounds 8 ounces at birth, what is the baby's weight in ounces?

Solution: 6 pounds $\times \dfrac{16 \text{ ounces}}{1 \text{ pound}}$ = 96 ounces; 96 + 8 = 104 ounces.

Example 33: We need 2 tons of dirt to fill a large hole. A truck can carry up to 900 pounds per truckload. The cost is $165 per truckload plus 2 cents a pound for the dirt. How much does it cost to fill the hole?

Solution: 2 tons $\times \dfrac{2000 \text{ pounds}}{1 \text{ ton}} =$ 4000 pounds. The number of truckloads is $\dfrac{4000}{900}$ = 4 truckloads + 400 pounds left over. Therefore, we need 5 trucks at $165 per truckload = 5 $\times$ $165 = $825. Additionally, we must pay 4000 pounds $\times$ .02 per pound = $80. So the total cost is $80 + $825 = $905.

TEMPERATURE

The United States uses the Fahrenheit scale: 32°F is the freezing temperature, and 212°F is the boiling point.

On the Celsius scale, 0°C is the freezing temperature, and 100°C is the boiling point.

The relationship between the scales is $F = \dfrac{9}{5}C + 32$, a formula that the TABE would probably give if it asked questions about the two scales.

Example 34: Use your calculator to find what 20°C and 37°C are on the Fahrenheit scale.

Solutions: $F = \dfrac{9}{5}C + 32 = \left(\dfrac{9}{5}\right)(20) + 32 = 68°$ F, a comfortable room temperature.

$F = \dfrac{9}{5}C + 32 = \left(\dfrac{9}{5}\right)(37) + 32 = 98.6°$ F, the normal body temperature.

Example 35: At what temperature do the two scales (Fahrenheit and Celsius) meet?

Solution: We want to know when $C = F$. Because $F = \dfrac{9}{5}C + 32$, we can write

$F = \dfrac{9}{5}F + 32$ by substituting F for C. Then, to solve,

$F = \dfrac{9}{5}F + 32$ — Multiply every term by 5

$5F = 9F + 160$ — Subtract $9F$ from both sides

$-4F = 160$ — Divide each side by -4

$F = -40°F$ — $-40°F = -40°C$

MISCELLANEOUS

Finally, let's look at a longer example that is presented for several reasons, mentioned at the end of the example.

Example 36: Change 90 miles per hour to feet per second.

Solution: $\dfrac{90 \text{ miles}}{\text{hour}} \times \dfrac{1 \text{ hour}}{60 \text{ minutes}} \times \dfrac{1 \text{ minute}}{60 \text{ seconds}} \times \dfrac{5280 \text{ feet}}{1 \text{ mile}} = 132\dfrac{\text{feet}}{\text{second}}$

This setup shows you whether to multiply or divide a certain equivalence because dimensions must cancel.

 Notes

1. Each of the last three fractions in the equation equals 1; when you multiply by 1, the number doesn't change.

2. Hours, minutes, and miles cancel. You are left with feet per second.

3. If the TABE asks you to do arithmetic like this, it would be by calculator.

If you drive a vehicle at 90 mph, and it takes 2 seconds to react, you would go 264 feet before you started to stop. If you were driving at 90 mph and were 400 feet (40 or so car lengths) from a brick wall when you started to brake, you would crash!

When I took my driving test centuries ago, we had to know these facts (not the arithmetic). You, however, need to know the arithmetic, but not the facts. But it would be nice if you remembered this when you drive.

The rest of this chapter is strictly for fun! If you don't like fun, go to the next chapter.

Question: Write in the order of heavy to light: a pound of feathers, a pound of gold, and a pound of caviar. Is this a trick question? Aren't they are all the same?

Answer: This *is* a trick question—they are all different!

The heaviest is feathers; there are 16 ounces to the pound.

In theory, a pound of caviar (not my taste) should weigh the same. However, if you order a "pound" of caviar, the usual jar is 14 ounces.

The lightest is gold. Precious metals like gold and platinum are measured on a different weight scale, called Troy measure. On the Troy scale, a pound is 12 ounces.

Not being greedy, I'll take the lightest pound! I'm sure you would also. (Pure gold is now somewhere around $900 an ounce, or about $11,000 a pound!)

Let's do some exercises.

Calculators are permitted for these exercises.

Exercise 1:   A quadrilateral with opposite sides parallel is defined as a

    A. Parallelogram   **C.** Rhombus

    B. Rectangle   **D.** Square

Exercise 2:   Which is *not* true about a rectangle?

    A. All angles are right angles.

    B. Diagonals bisect each other.

    C. Diagonals are congruent.

    D. Diagonals are perpendicular.

Exercise 3:   Which is the area of a square?

    A. $A = bh$ **C.** $A = \frac{1}{2}d^2$

    B. $A = s^2$ **D.** All of the above

Exercise 4:   The diagonals of which quadrilateral bisect each other, are congruent, and are perpendicular?

    A. Parallelogram   **C.** Rhombus

    B. Rectangle   **D.** Square

Exercise 5:   A line segment from one side of a circle to the other is defined as a

    A. Chord   **C.** Diameter

    B. Radius   **D.** Tangent

Exercise 6:   A line touching a circle in only one point is a

    A. Secant   **C.** Bisector

    B. Tangent   **D.** Radius

Exercise 7:   A rectangle with base 5 and height 8 has an area of

      A. 13   **C.** 26

      B. 20   **D.** 40

Exercise 8:   A rectangle with base 5 and height 8 has a perimeter of

      A. 13   **C.** 26

      B. 20   **D.** 40

Exercise 9:   A square has an area and perimeter that are numerically the same. The side is

      A. 4   **C.** 8

      B. 6   **D.** 10

Exercise 10:   A triangle has base 10 and area 40. Its height is

      A. 2   **C.** 6

      B. 4   **D.** 8

Exercise 11:   A circle has diameter 40; let $\pi = 3.14$. Its area is

      A. 60.28   **C.** 1256

      B. 120.56   **D.** 5024

Exercise 12:   A circle has diameter 40; let $\pi = 3.14$. Its circumference is

      A. 60.28   **C.** 1256

      B. 125.6   **D.** 5024

Exercise 13:   The area of a trapezoid is given by $A = \frac{1}{2}h(b_1 + b_2)$. If the bases are 8 and 10 and the height is 12, the area is

      A. 108   **C.** 300

      B. 216   **D.** 960

Exercise 14:   The perimeter of the trapezoid in Exercise 13 is

      A. 30   **C.** 960

      B. 42   **D.** Cannot be determined

Exercise 15: The volume of a cube with edge 10 is

       A. 30   **C.** 100

       B. 60   **D.** 1,000

Exercise 16: The front of a box has base 3 and height 4. If the width of the box is 10, its volume is

       A. 17   **C.** 120

       B. 34   **D.** 720

Exercise 17: The diagonal of the front of the box described in Exercise 16 is

       A. 5   **C.** 7

       B. 6   **D.** 12

Exercise 18: 23 meters are how many centimeters?

       A. .023   **C.** 2300

       B. 0.23   **D.** 23,000

Exercise 19: How many minutes are there in 2 days?

       A. 60   **C.** 2880

       B. 1440   **D.** 14,400

Exercise 20: 5 yards 4 feet 3 inches is how many inches?

       A. 12   **C.** 228

       B. $19\frac{1}{3}$ **D.** 231

Let's look at the answers

Answer 1:   A

Answer 2:   D

Answer 3:   D

Answer 4:   D

Answer 5:   A

Answer 6:   B

Answer 7:   D: $5 \times 8 = 40$.

Answer 8:   C: $5 + 8 + 5 + 8 = 26$.

Answer 9:   A: $4(4) = 4^2$.

Answer 10:   D: $A = \frac{1}{2}bh$; $40 = \frac{10}{2}h$; $5h = 40$; $h = \frac{40}{5} = 8$.

Answer 11:   C: $r = \frac{d}{2} = \frac{40}{2} = 20$;; $A = 3.14\,(20)(20) = 1256$.

Answer 12:   B: $C = 3.14d = 3.14(40) = 125.6$.

Answer 13:   A: $A = \frac{1}{2}(12)(18) = 108$.

Answer 14:   D: You do not know the lengths of all the sides.

Answer 15:   D: $10 \times 10 \times 10 = 1{,}000$.

Answer 16:   C: $3 \times 4 \times 10 = 120$.

Answer 17:   A: $\sqrt{3^2+4^2}=\sqrt{25}=5$.

Answer 18:   C: 23×100; when going from larger to smaller, you multiply.

Answer 19:   C: 2 days $\times\ \dfrac{24\text{ hours}}{1\text{ day}}\ \times\ \dfrac{60\text{ minutes}}{1\text{ hour}}=2880$.

Answer 20:   D: $(5\times 36)+(4\times 12)+3=180+48+3=231$.

Let's do some other stuff.

CHAPTER 8: *How to Present Data, Including Probability and Statistics*

"*At this point, your probability of success has greatly increased. This chapter is a combination of related topics. Let's start with the measures of central tendancy.*"

CENTRAL TENDENCY

People say that you can prove anything with statistics. You need to know what you are taking statistics of, how many in the group, and many other variables. Even then, depending on the "spin" you want, you can choose among three measures to describe the data and prove your point. These measures of central tendency are ways to find a "typical" value. The measures of central tendency are:

Mean: Add up the number of terms and divide the sum by the number of terms; that's the way your grades are usually determined in school.

Median: The middle term when the numbers are put in order from smallest to largest (or the other way around). For an odd number of terms, it is the middle term; for an even number, it's the mean of the middle two numbers.

Mode: The most common term; there can be one mode, two modes (bimodal), or any number of modes.

For the data consisting of the numbers 5, 6, 8, 9, 12, 12, and 18,

the mean is $\dfrac{5 + 6 + 8 + 9 + 12 + 12 + 18}{7} = \dfrac{70}{7} = 10$.

The median is 9. There are three numbers above 9 and three numbers below it.

The mode is 12. It is the most common number, appearing twice.

Note *Any one of these measures can be said to be representative of the data. Now can you see how you can prove anything with statistics?*

Example 1: Find the mean, median, and mode for the following group of numbers: 8, 10, 10, 16, 16, 18

Solution: Mean $= \dfrac{8 + 10 + 10 + 16 + 16 + 18}{6} = 13$.

There are an even number of numbers, so to find the median, we have to take the average of the middle two: $\frac{10 + 16}{2} = 13$.

The data are bimodal; the modes are 10 and 16, each appearing twice.

The TABE seems to love to ask questions from tables, charts, and graphs on the second part of the test. The table in the following example is called a **frequency table**.

Example 2:   Sandy has taken 10 tests. Here are the results and the frequency (how many times) the grade was obtained. Sandy was a pretty good student in this particular subject.

Grade	Number
100	4
98	3
95	2
86	1
Total	10

Find the mean, median, and mode of Sandy's quiz scores.

Solution:

The mean is the longest measure to compute:

$$\frac{4 \times 100 + 3 \times 98 + 2 \times 95 + 86}{10} = 97$$

The median is determined by putting all of the numbers in order, so we have 100, 100, 100, 100, 98, 98, 98, 95, 95, 86. The middle terms are 98 and 98, so the median is 98.

The mode is 100 because that is the most common score; there are four of them.

COUNTING

The **basic law of counting** says: "If you can do something in p ways, and a second thing in q ways, and a third thing in r ways, and so on, the total number of ways you can do the first thing, then the second thing, then the third thing , etc., is $p \times q \times r \times \ldots$

Example 3:   If you have a lunch choice of 5 sandwiches, 4 desserts, and 3 drinks, and you can have one of each, how many different meals could you choose?

Solution: You can choose from $(5)(4)(3) = 60$ different meals

Example 4:   How many ways can five people line up?

Solution: The first person can choose any of 5 places, but the next person has only the 4 choices left, and so on. So this is just $5 \times 4 \times 3 \times 2 \times 1 = 120$.

Example 5:   How many ways can 7 people occupy 3 seats on a bench?

Solution: Any one of 7 people can be in the first seat, then any one of 6 people can be in the second seat, and any one of 5 people can be in the third seat. The total number would be $(7)(6)(5) = 210$ ways.

Avoiding Duplicates

When we count how many ways to do A or B, we should be careful not to count any items that include both A and B, so we subtract them:

$$N(A \text{ or } B) = N(A) + N(B) - N(A \text{ and } B)$$

Example 6:   Thirty students take Shop or Auto Mechanics. If 20 took Auto Mechanics and 18 took Shop, and if each student took at least one of these courses, how many took *both* Shop and Auto Mechanics?

Solution: $N(S \text{ or } AM) = N(S) + N(AM) - N(S \text{ and } AM)$, or $30 = 20 + 18 - x$, so $x = 8$ took both courses.

Example 7:   Forty students take math or history. If 9 take both and 20 take history, how many students take math?

Solution: $N(M \text{ or } H) = N(M) + N(H) - N(\text{both})$, or $40 = x + 20 - 9$, so $x = 29$ take math.

PROBABILITY

The probability (*Pr*) of an event is the number of "good" outcomes divided by the total number of outcomes possible, or $Pr(\text{success}) = \frac{\text{good outcomes}}{\text{total outcomes}}$.

Example 8: Consider the following sets: {26 letters of the English alphabet}; vowels = {*a, e, i, o, u*}; consonants = {the rest of the letters}. What are the probabilities of choosing a vowel? a consonant? any letter? π?

Solution: $Pr(\text{vowel}) = \frac{5}{26}$; $Pr(\text{consonant}) = \frac{21}{26}$; $Pr(\text{letter}) = \frac{26}{26}$; $Pr(\pi) = \frac{0}{26} = 0$.

Probability follows the same rule about avoiding duplicates as discussed in the previous section.

$$Pr(A \text{ or } B) = Pr(A) + Pr(B) - Pr(A \text{ and } B)$$

Example 9: What is the probability that a spade or an ace is pulled from a 52-card deck?

Solution: $Pr(\text{Spade or ace}) = Pr(\text{Spade}) + Pr(\text{Ace}) - Pr(\text{Spade ace}) =$

$\frac{13}{52} + \frac{4}{52} - \frac{1}{52} = \frac{16}{52} = \frac{4}{13}$

As weird as it sounds, whenever I taught this in a class, I never failed to have at least two students who didn't know what a deck of cards was, and I taught in New York City!

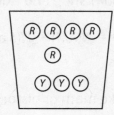

Use this figure for Examples 10 through 13. In the jar are 5 red balls and 3 yellow balls.

Example 10: Find the probability of picking a yellow ball.

Solution: There are 3 yellow balls and 8 total balls, so $Pr(\text{yellow}) = \frac{3}{8}$.

Example 11: Find the probability of picking a red ball.

Solution: There are 5 red balls and 8 total balls, so $Pr(\text{red}) = \frac{5}{8}$.

Example 12: What is the probability that two yellow balls are picked, with replacement?

Solution: Pr(2 yellow balls, with replacement) $= \left(\dfrac{3}{8}\right)\left(\dfrac{3}{8}\right) = \dfrac{9}{64}$.

Example 13: What is the probability of picking two yellow balls, without replacement?

Solution: The first yellow ball is not replaced, so for the second pick, there are only 7 balls, 2 of which are yellow. Pr(2 yellow balls, no replacement) $=$ $\left(\dfrac{3}{8}\right)\left(\dfrac{2}{7}\right) = \dfrac{3}{28}$.

Let's do a little on charts and graphs.

CHARTS AND GRAPHS

As mentioned before, the TABE seems to love tables and charts. The TABE will give you only one chart or table or graph and usually two or three questions about it. For these questions, there are a lot of calculations!

Here are two more graphics for Exercises 14 through 18. This problem is good practice. You should do all the calculations. A chart of the answers is provided with how to do all the calculations. On the actual TABE, the calculations may be as messy (because you have a calculator). However, there will be fewer calculations than here! On these examples, the multiple-choice answers are included.

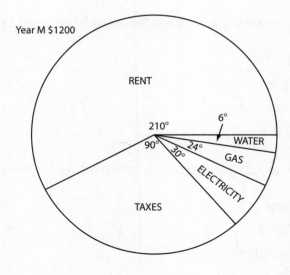

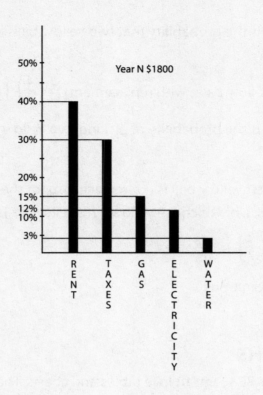

OK. Enough talking! Let's get started.

Some of the major expenses of the apartment of Mr. and Mrs. Smith in Smallville, USA, are shown in this pie chart and bar graph. The pie chart is for year M with a $1200 budget, and the bar graph is for year N, some years later, with an $1800 budget. Use these data for Examples 14 through 18.

Example 14: The smallest percentage increase from year M to year N is for

      A. Rent

      B. Taxes

      C. Electricity

      D. Gas

Example 15: The largest percentage increase from year *M* to year *N* is for

      A. Rent

      B. Taxes

      C. Electricity

      D. Gas

Example 16: The change in rent from year *M* to year *N* was

      A. −$80

      B. none

      C. +$20

      D. +$100

Example 17: The two closest monetary amounts are

      A. Rent in year *M* and the Rent in year *N*

      B. Electricity in year *M* and Gas in year *N*

      C. Water in year *M* and Water in year *N*

      D. Taxes in year *M* and Gas in year *N*

Example 18: Which expenses exceeded the percentage increase in the total budget?

      A. All the expenses

      B. All except Rent

      C. All except Water

      D. All except Water and Rent

These examples are easier to answer if we exactly calculate all of the money answers and put the items next to each other in a table:

	Year *M*	Year *N*
Rent	$\frac{210}{360} \times \$1200 = \frac{7}{12} \times \$1200 =$	$.40 \times \$1800 =$
	$700	$720
Taxes	$300	$540
Electricity	$100	$216
Gas	$80	$270
Water	$20	$54

Let's look at the solutions.

Solution 14: A: Rent increased by only $20 (due perhaps to rent control or family member owner); the percentage increase is the smallest increase (= $\frac{20}{700}$ × 100). You don't actually have to calculate the exact percentage. You only have to note the percentage increase is obviously much smaller than the percentage increase of any other item.

Solution 15: D: The percentage increase for gas is $\frac{190}{80}$ × 100%, or more than a 200% increase.

Solution 16: C: $720 − $700 = $20.

Solution 17: A: The rents in year M and year N are only $20 apart. No other choices are this close.

Solution 18: B: The total increase from year M to year N is 50%; taxes almost doubled; electricity more than doubled; gas more than tripled; and water almost tripled.

Sometimes the TABE gives you a picture on graph paper and asks questions about it. You should be able to count on the graph paper to see where these points are.

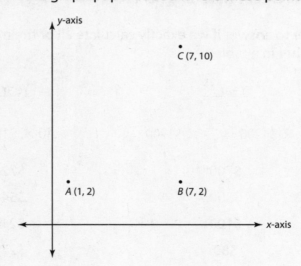

Example 19: Find the midpoint of AC.

Solution: We see that A is (1, 2) and C is (7, 10). Let (1, 2) = (x_1, y_1) and let (7, 10) = (x_2, y_2).

$$\text{Midpoint} = \left(\frac{x_1 + x_2}{2}, \frac{y_1 + y_2}{2}\right) = \left(\frac{1 + 7}{2}, \frac{2 + 10}{2}\right) = (4, 6)$$

Example 20: Find the length of *AC*.

Solution: Again, *A* is (1, 2) and *C* is (7, 10). We can use two methods to find the length of *AC*.

Method 1:

$$\text{Length} = \sqrt{(x_2 - x_1)^2 + (y_2 - y_1)^2} = \sqrt{(7-1)^2 + (10-2)^2} = \sqrt{6^2 + 8^2} = \sqrt{100} = 10$$

Method 2: Look at the graph! We see that $\triangle ABC$ is a right triangle. If we count the boxes, we see that *AB* is length 6 and *BC* is length 8. If we remember our Pythagorean triples, we know *AC* = 10!

Example 21: Find the area of $\triangle ABC$.

Solution: Because $\triangle ABC$ is a right triangle, we can call *AB* the base, $b = 6$, and *BC* the height, $h = 8$. The area of the triangle is $A = \frac{1}{2}bh = \left(\frac{1}{2}\right)(6)(8) = 24$ square units.

Note *Notice that the perimeter $p = 6 + 8 + 10 = 24$ units.*

TRANSLATIONS

Translations are movements up or down, or left or right, or any combination of them.

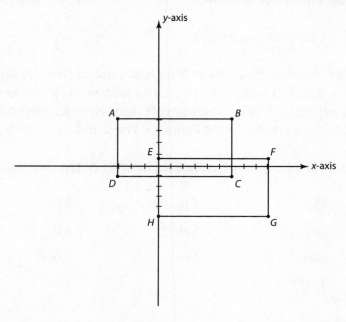

Notice in this figure that rectangle *EFGH* is a translation of rectangle *ABCD*. The rectangle has movement 3 to the right and 4 units down. To answer Examples 22 to 25, you should first determine the points from the graph. Points $A(-3, 5)$, $B(6, 5)$, $C(6, -1)$, and $D(-3, -1)$ form rectangle *ABCD*. Points $E(0, 1)$, $F(9, 1)$, $G(9, -5)$, and $H(0, -5)$ form rectangle *EFGH*.

Example 22: Find the area of *ABCD*.

Solution: $A = bh = (9)(6) = 54$ square units

Example 23: Find the perimeter of *ABCD*.

Solution: $p = 2b + 2h = 2(9) + 2(6) = 30$ units

Example 24: Find the area of *EFGH*.

Solution: $A = bh = (9)(6) = 54$ square units

Example 25: Find the perimeter of *EFGH*.

Solution: $p = 2b + 2h = 2(9) + 2(6) = 30$ units

Note *The area and perimeter do not change with a translation. Only the position changes.*

Q Let's do some exercises.

Calculators are permitted for these exercises.

For Exercises 1–8, use the following scenario:

RAM has 20 Famous Fast Food restaurants in the great state of New Jersey. His foods are named for some in his extended family. There are the following: Burt's Bountiful Burgers, Charles's Choice Cheeseburgers, Wally's Wonderful Wings (sold by the half dozen), Sam's Superb Salads, Frank's Fabulous Franks, Fran's Fantastic Fries, and Sandra's Scrumptious Sodas.

Over the past 16 years, this is how many were sold in units of ten thousand.

Hamburgers	480	Cheeseburgers	320
Wings	200	Salads	240
Franks	600	Fries	2,400
Sodas	3,400		

Exercise 1: How many hamburgers were sold?

A. 480

B. 480,000

C. 4,800,000

D. 48,000,000

Exercise 2: How many wings were sold?

A. 200

B. 200,000

C. 2,000,000

D. 20, 000,000

Exercise 3: The average number of fries sold per year was

A. 150

B. 150,000

C. 1,500,000

D. 15,000,000

Exercise 4: All foods are sold with a 25% increase from total cost. If Burt's Bountiful Burgers sells for three dollars, the total cost of a burger was

A. $2.40

B. $2.50

C. $3.25

D. $3.75

Exercise 5: All the drinks are marked up 200%. If the huge Sandra's Scrumptious Soda sells for $1.50, its original cost was

A. $ 0.50

B. $ 0.75

C. $3.00

D. $4.50

Exercise 6: The average number of Charles's Choice Cheeseburgers per restaurant per year is

A. 10,000

B. 200,000

C. 160,000

D. 320,000

Exercise 7: John ordered a special: two Burt's Bountiful Burgers and one huge Sandra's Scrumptious Soda for $6.00. The percentage saving over buying them separately was

A. 1.50

B. 15

C. 20

D. 25

Exercise 8:   The cost of Sam's Superb Salad is $2.00. If all foods are sold with a 25% increase, the selling price is

A. $2.40   C. $2.75

B. $2.50   D. $3.00

Exercises 9–11 refer to the set of numbers {9, 2 , 2, 5, 6, 10, 10}.

Exercise 9:   The mean is closest to

A. 5   C. 7

B. 6   D. There is no mean

Exercise 10:   The median is

A. 5   C. 6

B. 5.5   D. 10

Exercise 11:   The mode is

A. 5   C. 10

B. 5.5   D. There are two of them

For Exercises 12 and 13, consider the set {1, 5, 6, 7, 8, 9}.

Exercise 12:   How many different three-digit numbers can you make from this set (repeats allowed)?

A. 240   C. 120

B. 216   D. 60

Exercise 13:   How many three-digit numbers can you make with no repeating digits?

A. 240   C. 180

B. 216   D. 120

For Exercises 14–17, use the following information: a bowl contains 7 red balls and 3 blue balls.

Exercise 14: One ball is picked; the probability it won't be blue is

    A. $\dfrac{3}{7}$ **C.** $\dfrac{7}{10}$

    B. $\dfrac{7}{3}$ **D.** $\dfrac{3}{10}$

Exercise 15: Two balls are picked with replacement; the probability that both are blue is

    A. 0.3   **C.** 0.03

    B. 0.9   **D.** 0.09

Exercise 16: Two balls are picked without replacement; the probability that both are red is

    A. $\dfrac{1}{2}$ **C.** $\dfrac{49}{100}$

    B. $\dfrac{7}{15}$ **D.** $\dfrac{2}{5}$

Exercise 17: The probability that one ball picked is not green is

    A. 0   **C.** 1

    B. $\dfrac{1}{2}$ **D.** None of these

Exercise 18: Given the point (1, 2), if you move it 4 to the right, down 5, and then left 7, the new point is

    A. (2, 3)   **C.** (2, −3)

    B. (−2, 3)   **D.** (−2, −3)

Exercise 19: Everyone takes either math or history. If 40 take math or history, 30 take math, and 25 take history, how many take both?

    A. 5   **C.** 15

    B. 10   **D.** 20

Exercise 20: For lunch, you have a choice of 10 different sandwiches, 8 different desserts and 6 different drinks. The total number of different meals you may have is

A. 6   C. 480

B. 24   D. Infinite

 Let's look at the answers

Answer 1:   C: Units of 10,000, so 480 × 10,000 = 4,800,000

Answer 2:   C: 200 × 10,000 = 2,000,000

Answer 3:   C: 2400 × 10,000 ÷ 16 (number of years) = 1,500,000

Answer 4:   A: A 25% increase means 100% + 25% = 125% = 1.25, so we use

$$\frac{\$3.00}{1.25} = \$2.40$$

Answer 5:   A: A 200% markup means 100% + 200% = 300% = 3.00, so

$$\frac{\$1.50}{3.00} = \$0.50$$

Answer 6:   A: 320 × 10,000 ÷ 20 (per restaurant) ÷ 16 (per year) = 10,000

Answer 7:   C: The total cost would be 2($3.00) + $1.50 = $7.50; $7.50 − $6.00 = $1.50 difference, so the percentage saving would be $\frac{1.50}{7.50} \times 100\% = 20\%$

Answer 8:   B: $2.00 + .25(2.00) = $2.50

Answer 9:   B: $(9 + 2 + 2 + 5 + 6 + 10 + 10) = \frac{44}{7} = 6.3$, which is closest to 6

Answer 10:   C: The middle one is 6

Answer 11:   D: There are two modes, 2 and 10

Answer 12:   B: $6 \times 6 \times 6 = 216$

Answer 13:   D: $6 \times 5 \times 4 = 120$

Answer 14:   C

Answer 15:   D: $\dfrac{3}{10} \times \dfrac{3}{10} = \dfrac{9}{100} = .09$

Answer 16:   B: $\dfrac{7}{10} \times \dfrac{6}{9} = \dfrac{7}{15}$

Answer 17:   C: There is a 100% chance that the ball is not green because there are only red and blue balls

Answer 18:   D

Answer 19:   C: 40 (math or history) = 30 (math) + 25 (history) − x (both math and history); $x = 15$

Answer 20:   C: $10 \times 8 \times 6 = 480$

Let's go to the chapter that contains all the remaining stuff.

CHAPTER 9: *Properties of Numbers and Patterns*

"To know the plan, patterns and properties will help you succeed."

PROPERTIES OF NUMBERS

The TABE asks questions about some of the rules of numbers, so it's good to know what they are. In Chapter 4, we already talked about the Distributive Property.

Commutative Property of Addition: For any numbers, a and b, $a + b = b + a$. You can add numbers in either order, and get the same sum. $3 + 7 = 7 + 3 = 10$.

Commutative Property of Multiplication: For any numbers, a and b, $a \times b = b \times a$. You can multiply in either order and get the same product. $7(4) = 4(7) = 28$.

Notes

1. Subtraction is **not** commutative because $5 - 6 \neq$ (**does not equal**) $6 - 5$.

2. Division is **not** commutative because $7 \div 3 \neq 3 \div 7$.

Associative Property of Addition: For all numbers a, b, and c, $(a + b) + c = a + (b + c)$. You can add the first two and then the third or add the first to the sum of the last two, and the total sum on each side will be the same. $(7 + 5) + 2 = 7 + (5 + 2) = 14$.

Associative Property of Multiplication: $(ab)c = a(bc)$: You can multiply the first two numbers and then multiply the third or multiply the first to the product of the last two and the answer will be the same. $(10 \times 4) \times 3 = 10 \times (4 \times 3) = 120$.

Distributive Property of Multiplication over Addition: $a(b + c) = ab + ac$; $4(x + 6) = 4x + 24$.

Distributive Property of Multiplication over Subtraction: $a(b - c) = ab - ac$; $8(2x - 3) = 16x - 24$.

Example 1:   Write the properties for each of the equalities.

Problems	Solutions
a. $5(9) = 9(5)$	Commutative property of multiplication
b. $9 + 6 = 6 + 9$	Commutative property of addition
c. $4(3 + 6) = 12 + 24$	Distributive property of multiplication over addition
d. $7(9 - x) = 63 - 7x$	Distributive property of multiplication over subtraction
e. $(5 \times 6) \times 7 = 5 \times (6 \times 7)$	Associative property of multiplication
f. $1 + (2 + 4) = (1 + 2) + 4$	Associative property of addition
g. $4(x - 5) = (x - 5)4$	Commutative property of multiplication (not distributive law—the order of multiplication has changed)
h. $5 + (6 + 2) = (6 + 2) + 5$	Commutative property of addition (not associative property—the order of addition has switched!)

PATTERNS

I've saved the most fun for last. Sometimes the TABE asks you to identify patterns. Sometimes it's number patterns, and sometimes it's picture patters. Let look at a few.

Example 2:   Find the next two numbers: 2, 5, 8, 11, ___, ___.

Solution: Here we can see the difference between consecutive terms is 3. The next two numbers are 14 and 17.

Note *On the TABE, the answers will be multiple choices.*

Example 3:   Find the next two numbers: 80, 40, 20, ___, ___.

Solution: Here each term is divided by 2 to get the next term; so the next two numbers are 10 and 5, in that order.

Example 4:   Find the next two numbers: 1, −2, 3, −4, 5, __, __.

Solution: Here the numbers are going in order but alternating signs. The next two numbers are −6 and 7.

Let's try a couple of examples that are a little harder.

Example 5:   Fill in the two missing numbers: 1, 4, 9, __, __ 36, 49.

Solution: There are two ways to look at this one. First, the difference $4 - 1 = 3$; the difference $9 - 4 = 5$; the differences are increasing by 2; so $9 + 7 = 16$ is the next one; $16 + 9 = 25$ is the next one; notice $25 + 11 = 36$, the next one; and finally $36 + 13 = 49$ is the last one. The second way is to notice that $1^2 = 1$, $2^2 = 4$, $3^2 = 9$; so the next one is $4^2 = 16$, $5^2 = 25$; notice $6^2 = 36$, and $7^2 = 49$.

Example 6:   Fill in the next two numbers: 0, 1, 1, 2, 3, 5, 8, __, __

Solution: The next two numbers are 13 and 21. This is a very special sequence called the **Fibonacci** sequence. You get the third term by adding the first two. You get any term after the third by adding the previous two: $0 + 1 = 1$, $1 + 1 = 2$, $1 + 2 = 3$, $2 + 3 = 5$, and $3 + 5 = 8$. So $5 + 8 = 13$ and $8 + 13 = 21$ are the next two.

Last, we have picture patterns.

Example 7:

In this sequence of pictures, what would the next one look like?

Solution: The fourth picture in the sequence would be a darkened square in the lower left.

Example 8:

Picture 9–2:

What would the next two pictures look like?

Solution: The fourth line would be a triangle followed by a darkened square followed by a triangle followed by a darkened square. The fifth line would be a square, then a dark triangle, then a square, then a dark triangle, then a square.

Picture 9–2:

Let's do some exercises.

Calculators are permitted for these exercises.

For Exercises 1–10, use the following key in seeing which the correct rules are.

1   **Commutative law with respect to addition**

2   **Commutative law with respect to multiplication**

3   **Associative law with respect to addition**

4   **Associative law with respect to multiplication**

5   **Distributive law over addition**

6   **Distributive law over subtraction**

Exercise 1: $4(3x - 12) = 12x - 48$

A. 3   C. 5

B. 4   D. 6

Exercise 2: $(4 + b) + c = 4 + (b + c)$

           A. 1   **C.** 3

           B. 2   **D.** 4

Exercise 3: $(ma)x = m(ax)$

           A. 1   **C.** 3

           B. 2   **D.** 4

Exercise 4: $a(a + d) = a^2 + ad$

           A. 3   **C.** 5

           B. 4   **D.** 6

Exercise 5: $em = me$

           A. 1   **C.** 3

           B. 2   **D.** 4

Exercise 6: $p + t = t + p$

           A. 1   **C.** 2

           B. 2   **D.** 4

Exercise 7: $p(b - c) = (b - c)p$

           A. 1   **C.** 5

           B. 2   **D.** 6

Exercise 8: $(a + b) + c = c + (a + b)$

           A. 1   **C.** 3

           B. 2   **D.** 4

Exercise 9: $(lo)x = x(lo)$

           A. 1   **C.** 3

           B. 2   **D.** 4

Exercise 10: $(m + 6)r = r(m + 6)$

    A. 1   C. 5

    B. 2   D. 6

For Exercises 11–20, fill in the two missing terms in the sequence.

Exercise 11: 5, 14, 23, 32, 41, ___, ___, 68

    A. 52, 61   C. 50, 59

    B. 51, 60   D. 49, 60

Exercise 12: 12, 7, 2, −3, ___, ___, −18

    A. −5, −10   C. −7, −11

    B. −5, −12   D. −8, −13

Exercise 13: 1, 2, 4, 8, ___, ___, 64

    A. 12, 32   C. 10, 30

    B. 12, 24   D. 16, 32

Exercise 14: 5, −3, 8, −5, 11, −7, ___, ___, 17, −11

    A. 13, −10   C. 14, −9

    B. 13, −9   D. 14, −10

Exercise 15: 0, 1, 1, 2, 3, 5, 8, ___, ___, 34

    A. 15, 19   C. 14, 25

    B. 13, 21   D. 15, 24

Exercise 16: *b, f, j, n,* ___, ___, *z*

    A. *r, v*   C. *p, u*

    B. *s, w*   D. *s, u*

Exercise 17: 3, 6, 11, 18, 27, ___, ___, 66

           A. 35, 45   **C.** 39, 49

           B. 38, 51   **D.** 40, 52

Exercise 18: 480, −240, 120, −60, ___, ___, 7.5

           A. 80, −30   **C.** 28, −12.75

           B. 30, −15   **D.** 25, −18

Exercise 19: 11, 6, ___, ___, −9, −14

           A. 1, −5   **C.** −1, −4

           B. 1, −4   **D.** 1, −6

Exercise 20: 400, 40, 4, ___, ___, 0.004, 0.0004

           A. 0, .04   **C.** 1, .04

           B. 1, .4   **D.** .4, .04

 Let's look at the answers

Answer 1: D

Answer 2: C

Answer 3: D

Answer 4: C

Answer 5: B

Answer 6: A

Answer 7: B: The order of multiplication changes.

Answer 8: A: The order of addition changes.

Answer 9:   B: The order of multiplication changes.

Answer 10:   B: The order of multiplication changes.

Answer 11:   C: The rule is add 9.

Answer 12:   D: Subtract 5.

Answer 13:   D: Multiply by 2.

Answer 14:   C: Add 3 to the positive terms; then subtract 2 from the negative ones.

Answer 15:   B: $0 + 1 = 1, 1 + 1 = 2, 1 + 2 = 3, 2 + 3 = 5, 3 + 5 = 8, 5 + 8 = 13, 8 + 13 = 21$, and finally $13 + 21 = 34$; these are called Fibonacci numbers.

Answer 16:   A: The letters are 4 apart in the alphabet.

Answer 17:   B: $(6 - 3) = 3; (11 - 6) = 5; (18 - 11) = 7; (27 - 18) = 9$; so $(38 - 27) = 11$ and $(51 - 38) = 13$; finally $(66 - 51) = 15$; the differences increase by 2, a toughie.

Answer 18:   B: The terms are divided by -2 or multiplied by $-\frac{1}{2}$.

Answer 19:   B: The terms reduce by 5.

Answer 20:   D: The terms are divided by 10.

Now let's try to practice all of our skills.

"*For total success, you must practice your skills.* "

Part I: Mathematics Computation

Note *No calculator permitted.*

1. $\sqrt{81} - \sqrt{49} =$

    A 2   **D** 18

    B $\sqrt{32}$ **E** None of these

    C 16

2. $3^2 \times 4^1 =$

    A 36   **D** 144

    B 48   **E** None of these

    C 72

3. $\frac{3}{4} \times 6 =$

    A $\frac{1}{4}$ **D** $\frac{9}{2}$

    B $\frac{1}{24}$ **E** None of these

    C $\frac{9}{4}$

4. $\dfrac{24}{-6}$

    A −144   **D** 18

    B −4   **E** None of these

    C 4

5. 20% of 40 =

    A 2   **D** 80

    B 8   **E** None of these

    C 20

6. $\dfrac{3}{4} + \dfrac{5}{6} =$

    A $\dfrac{3}{8}$

    B $\dfrac{4}{5}$

    C $1\dfrac{7}{12}$

    D $2\dfrac{7}{12}$

    E None of these

7. If $3x = 24$, $x =$

    A 8   **D** 72

    B 21   **E** None of these

    C 27

8. 3045 =

   A $3 \times 10^2 + 4 \times 10 + 5$

   B $3 \times 10^3 + 4 \times 10 + 5$

   C $3 \times 10^4 + 4 \times 10^2 + 5$

   D $3 \times 10^2 + 4 \times 10 + 5 \times 10^{-1}$

   E None of these

9. $\dfrac{.0072}{.0008} =$

   A 0.9   **D** 900

   B 9   **E** None of these

   C 90

10. $(4^2 - 3^2)^2 =$

    A 1   **D** 127

    B 4   **E** None of these

    C 49

11. $4(x^2 - 5) =$

    A $4x^2 - 20$ **D** $4x^2 - 9$

    B $16x^2 - 20$ **E** None of these

    C $4x^2 - 5$

12. $\dfrac{3}{5} \div \dfrac{7}{2} =$

    A $\dfrac{21}{10}$ **D** 7

    B $\dfrac{6}{35}$ **E** None of these

    C $\dfrac{41}{10}$

13. $4\frac{3}{8} + 4\frac{1}{2} =$

    A $8\frac{7}{8}$ **D** $9\frac{2}{5}$

    B $9\frac{7}{8}$ **E** None of these

    C $8\frac{2}{5}$

14. 45% of $x = 90$; $x =$

    A 20   **D** 405

    B 200   **E** None of these

    C 40.5

15. $6 + 40 \div 4 - 16 =$

    A 44   **D** $-4\frac{1}{2}$

    B $2\frac{1}{2}$ **E** None of these

    C 0

16. $x - 7 = 11$; $x =$

    A $-\frac{11}{7}$ **D** 77

    B 4   **E** None of these

    C 18

17. $.00073 =$

    A 7.3×10^{-2} **D** 7.3×10^{-5}

    B 7.3×10^{-3} **E** None of these

    C 7.3×10^{-4}

18. $\sqrt{100} =$

      A 50   **D** 10

      B 25   **E** None of these

      C 20

19. 8% of 8 is

      A 64   **D** 0.064

      B 6.4   **E** None of these

      C 0.64

20. $3\overline{)44.4} =$

      A 0.148   **D** 148

      B 1.48   **E** None of these

      C 14.8

21. $^-8 \times\ ^-12 =$

      A −20   **D** 96

      B 20   **E** None of these

      C −96

22. $7 -\ ^-4 =$

      A −3   **D** 28

      B 3   **E** None of these

      C 11

23. $\dfrac{12}{7} \div 2 =$

    A $\dfrac{24}{7}$ **D** $\dfrac{10}{7}$

    B $\dfrac{6}{7}$ **E** None of these

    C 2

24. What % of $40 is $24.00?

    A 20%   **D** 80%

    B 40%   **E** None of these

    C 60%

25. $6^4 6^6 =$

    A 6^{10} **D** 36^{24}

    B 36^{10} **E** None of these

    C 6^{24}

26. $0.33 - 0.117 =$

    A 0.227   **D** 0.213

    B 0.217   **E** None of these

    C 0.223

27. $\dfrac{0}{7} - 0(7) - 7 =$

    A 0   **D** -21

    B -7 **E** None of these

    C -14

28. $1\dfrac{2}{3} - \dfrac{3}{4} =$

    A $2\dfrac{5}{12}$ **D** $\dfrac{5}{12}$

    B $1\dfrac{5}{12}$ **E** None of these

    C $\dfrac{11}{12}$

29. $\frac{4}{5} \div 4$

    A $\frac{16}{5}$ **D** $\frac{1}{5}$

    B $\frac{5}{16}$ **E** None of these

    C 5

30. $8 - {}^-2 =$

    A 10   **D** −6

    B −10   **E** None of these

    C 6

31. $\frac{1.62}{.006}$

    A 0.27   **D** 270

    B 2.7   **E** None of these

    C 27

32. 3 is what percent of 4?

    A $133\frac{1}{3}\%$ **D** $66\frac{2}{3}\%$

    B 80%

    C 75%   **E** None of these

33. $3 - 2^3 =$

    A 1   **D** −5

    B −1   **E** None of these

    C −3

34. $46.4 + .259 =$

       A 71.3   **D** 46.4259

       B 48.99   **E** None of these

       C 46.659

35. $(-1)^{10} =$

       A 1   **D** −10

       B −1   **E** None of these

       C 10

36. $(^-4 - 5) \times {}^-3 =$

       A 27   **D** −60

       B 11   **E** None of these

       C −3

37. $4.3 \times 10^{-5} =$

       A 0.43   **D** 0.00043

       B 0.043   **E** None of these

       C 0.0043

38. $\frac{1}{2} \times \frac{2}{3} \times \frac{3}{4} =$

       A $\frac{1}{3}$ **D** $\frac{1}{12}$

       B $\frac{1}{4}$ **E** None of these

       C $\frac{1}{6}$

39. $\dfrac{x^6}{x^2} =$

    A $\dfrac{1}{x^4}$ D x^4

    B $\dfrac{1}{x^3}$ E None of these

    C x^3

40. $\dfrac{-560}{-8} =$

    A 70   D -70

    B 7   E None of these

    C -7

Part II: Applied Mathematics

 *Calculators are permitted.*

1. Driving at 45 miles per hour, Al started at 2 p.m. and arrived at 4:20 p.m. on the same day. How far did Al travel?

    A 100 miles   C 110 miles

    B 105 miles   D 115 miles

2. Rounding 76.543 to the nearest tenth gives

    A 77.0   C 76.6

    B 76.5   D 76.54

3. Bob bought a meal for $38.50 plus a 20% tip. His total cost was

    A $45.00   C $46.20

    B $45.10   D $47.30

4. Chrissie had 3 red socks, 4 blue socks, and 8 white socks. If she picked one sock, what is the probability that one sock is red or white?

A $\dfrac{24}{96}$ C $\dfrac{11}{15}$

B $\dfrac{3}{8}$ D 1

5. Which equation means the same as 7 less than three times a number n is 27?

A $7 - 3n = 27$ C $7n - 3 = 27$

B $7n + 3 = 27$ D $3n - 7 = 27$

6. The number missing from the sequence 2, 3, 6, 11, ___, 27, 38 is

A 18   C 22

B 20   D 24

For problems 7–12, use the following circle with Center M.

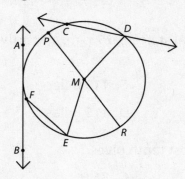

7. A diameter is

A AM C PR

B CD D Line through CD

8. A radius is

A EM C PR

B CD D Line through CD

9. One chord is

    A Line through *CD*   **C** *AM*

    B Line through *AB*   **D** *PR*

10. The line through points *C* and *D* is a

    A Tangent   **C** Chord

    B Secant   **D** Diameter

11. The line segment *CD* is a

    A Tangent   **C** Chord

    B Secant   **D** Diameter

12. If $PR = 16$ inches, the circumference $C = 2\pi r$, where $\pi = 3.14$, to the nearest inch is

    A 25   **C** 50

    B 26   **D** 51

13. Which is equivalent to $2x + 4y > 8$?

    A $x > 2y - 4$ **C** $x > 2y + 4$

    B $x > -2y + 4$ **D** $x > -2y - 4$

14. Light travels at 11,160,000 miles per minute. In 15 hours, approximately how far does light travel, in miles?

    A 10   **C** 10^8

    B 10^4 **D** 10^{10}

15. Dan cut a board into $1\frac{1}{4}$-foot pieces. How many full $1\frac{1}{4}$-foot pieces can be cut from a 28-foot board?

    A 20   **C** 22

    B 21   **D** 23

16. Interest $i = prt$, where p = the principal, r is the interest rate, and t = time. If Edie got $20 interest for investing $2000 at 4%, how long was the money in the bank?

    A 1 month   **C** 6 months

    B 3 months   **D** 1 year

For problems 17–20, use the following chart with Frank's 16 grades.

Grade	How Many
80	5
90	4
85	3
100	2
95	2

17. The median is

    A 80   C 85

    B 82.5   D 87.5

18. The mode is

    A 80   C 85

    B 82.5   D 100

19. The mean is closest to

    A 82   C 88

    B 85   D 91

20. The range is the largest value minus the smallest value. On this chart, the range is

    A 5   C 15

    B 10   D 20

21. At Gerri's workplace, the ratio of men to women is 3:4. If there are 84 workers, the number of women is

    A 36   C 48

    B 42   D 54

For problems 22–27, use the following graph.

Average Daily Temp
_____ **City *A***
_ _ _ _ _ _ _ **City *B***

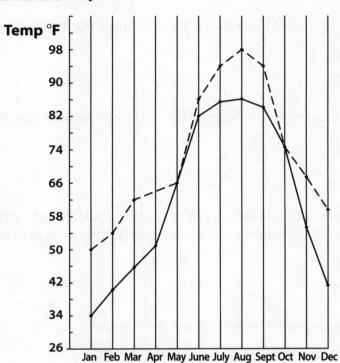

22. The average temperature in city *A* in February is about how many degrees?

   A 34   **C** 50

   B 40   **D** 54

23. The month of greatest temperature difference between city *A* and city *B* occurs in

   A January   **C** August

   B February   **D** December

24. The average (mean) difference in temperature for the months between the two months in which the temperatures for city *A* and city *B* are the same is about

    A $5\frac{2}{3}°$ **C** 8.5°

    B 6.8°   **D** 14°

25. The percentage increase in temperature in January from city *A* to city *B* is closest to

    A 16   **C** 47

    B 32   **D** 53

26. The percentage decrease in temperature in December from city *B* to city *A* is

    A 20   **C** $33\frac{1}{3}$

    B 25   **D** 40

27. At 60° F, you need a 15 SPF sunscreen to protect yourself. For each 5° increase, you need to increase the SPF by 3. In August in city *B*, what SPF is needed, to the nearest integer?

    A 30   **C** 38

    B 35   **D** 40

28. Which triplet represents the sides of a right triangle?

    A 4 − 5 − 6   **C** 4 − 7 − 10

    B 3 − 8 − 11   **D** 5 − 12 − 13

29. If $4x − 7 = 2x − 13$, $x =$

    A −10   **C** 3

    B −3   **D** 10

30. ABC Rent-A-Car has 400 cars, and $\frac{2}{5}$ are black. If they want to replace 25% of the black cars with silver cars, how many of the cars will remain black?

    A 40   **C** 120

    B 80   **D** 160

For problems 31–34, use the points on the following grid.

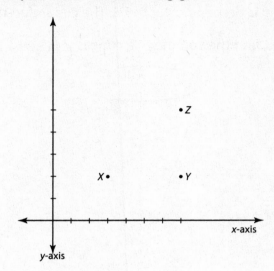

31. The coordinates of point *X* are

 A (2, 3)   **C** (⁻3, 2)

 B (3, 2)   **D** (3, ⁻2)

32. The midpoint of *XZ* is

 A (5, 2)   **C** (5, 3.5)

 B (7, 3.5)   **D** 8.5

33. The length of *XZ* is

 A 3   **C** 5

 B 4   **D** 7

34. The area of Δ*XYZ* =

 A 6   **C** 12

 B 9   **D** 24

35. In a recipe, for every 2 cups of flour, we use $\frac{1}{3}$ cup of butter. For 7 cups of flour, we need how many cups of butter?

 A 1   **C** $1\frac{1}{3}$

 B $1\frac{1}{6}$ **D** $1\frac{1}{2}$

For problems 36–39, use the following figure of a cone. *A* is the center of the circle, *DE* = 6 inches and *AB* = 4 inches. *AB* is perpendicular to *DE*. The circumference of a circle is $C = 2\pi r$; the area of a circle is $A = \pi r^2$, and the volume of a cone is $V = \frac{1}{3}\pi r^2 h$, where $\pi = 3.14$.

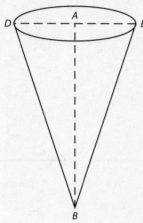

36. To the nearest square inch, the area of the circle is

    A 28   **C** 56

    B 29   **D** 57

37. To the nearest inch, the circumference of the circle is

    A 19   **C** 38

    B 29   **D** 39

38. To the nearest cubic inch, the volume of the cone is

    A 37   **C** 113

    B 38   **D** 114

39. The length in inches of *BE* is

    A 5   **C** 7

    B 6   **D** 10

40. Write the expression, "Your age *x* must be at least 18 to vote."

    A $x > 18$ **C** $x \leq 18$

    B $x \geq 18$ **D** $x < 18$

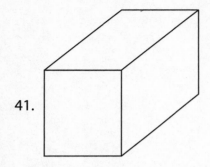

41.

A box is 1 foot long by 7 inches wide by 8 inches high. The volume in cubic inches is

    A 56   **C** 672

    B 560   **D** 1120

42. What value of x makes $\frac{3}{2}x + 10 = 22$?

    A 8   **C** 12

    B 10   **D** $21\frac{1}{3}$

43. At a family dinner for 30 people, there were 19 females. Of the 16 children, 10 were female children. How many were male and not children?

    A 3   **C** 7

    B 5   **D** 9

44. 222 ounces is closest to how many quarts?

    A 2   **C** 4

    B 3   **D** 7

45. A $33 sweater is marked down 25%. Harriett pays

    A $24.75   **C** $25.25

    B $25   **D** $25.75

46.

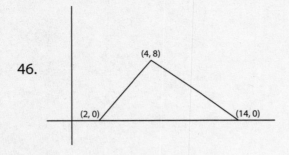

The area of this triangle is

      A 12   **C** 48

      B 24   **D** 96

47. A five-sided figure is called a

      A Quadrilateral   **C** Hexagon

      B Pentagon   **D** Dodecagon

48. After a 40% increase, a shirt cost $30.80. Originally, it cost

      A $20   **C** $24

      B $22   **D** $26

49. What number is a common factor of 24, 36, 27, and 12?

      A 2   **C** 4

      B 3   **D** 6

50. If you read from page 20 through page 45, how many pages did you read?

      A 25   **C** 65

      B 26   **D** 66

Practice Test 1, Part I Answers

1. A: $9 - 7 = 2$.

2. A: $9(4) = 36$.

3. D: $\frac{3}{4} \times \frac{6}{1} = \frac{18}{4} = \frac{9}{2}$. You could also cancel by first dividing the 4 and 6 by 2: $\frac{3}{2} \times 3 = \frac{9}{2}$.

4. B: $\frac{24}{6} = 4$; one minus sign means the answer is minus.

5. B: $.2 \times 40 = 8.0$.

6. C: $\frac{9}{12} + \frac{10}{12} = \frac{19}{12} = 1\frac{7}{12}$.

7. A: Divide both sides by 3.

8. B: Note that there is no 10^2 term.

9. B: You don't have to divide the decimal; you only need to locate the decimal point and move it 4 places to the right, top, and bottom: $\frac{72}{9} = 8$.

10. C: $16 - 9 = 7$, and $7^2 = 49$.

11. A: $4(x^2 - 5) = 4(x^2) + 4(-5) = 4x^2 - 20$.

12. B: Change to $\frac{3}{5} \times \frac{2}{7}$; multiply the tops and multiply the bottoms.

13. A: $4\frac{3}{8} + 4\frac{4}{8} = 8\frac{7}{8}$.

14. B: $\frac{90}{.45} = 200$.

15. C: $6 + 10 - 16 = 0$.

16. C: Add 7 to both sides.

17. C: Four places are needed from the location of the decimal point.

18. D

19. C: $.08 \times 8 = .64$.

20. C: Just locate the decimal point correctly.

21. D: $8 \times 12 = 96$; the product of two negatives is positive.

22. C: $7 + 4 = 11$.

23. B: $\frac{12}{7} \times \frac{1}{2} = \frac{6}{7}$.

24. C: $\dfrac{24}{40} = \dfrac{6}{10} = 60\%$.

25. A: Add the exponents; the base stays the same.

26. D: $0.330 - 0.117 = 0.213$; align the decimal points.

27. B: $0 - 0 - 7 = -7$.

28. C: $1\dfrac{8}{12} - \dfrac{9}{12}$ or $\dfrac{20}{12} - \dfrac{9}{12} = \dfrac{11}{12}$.

29. D: $\dfrac{4}{5} \times \dfrac{1}{4} = \dfrac{1}{5}$; the 4's cancel.

30. A: $-(-2) = +2$, so $8 + 2 = 10$.

31. D: Locate the decimal; this is the same as $\dfrac{1620}{6} = 270$.

32. C: $\dfrac{3}{4} = 75\%$.

33. D: $3 - 8 = -5$.

34. C: Line up the decimal points: $46.400 + .259 = 46.659$.

35. A: Any time you multiply ones you get 1; an even number of minus signs = plus.

36. A: $(-9)(-3) = +27$.

37. E: An exponent of -5 on base 10 means to move the decimal point 5 places to the left: .000043. This is not one of the answer choices. On this test, only 1 or 2 answers are ever choice E.

38. B: The 2's and 3's cancel.

39. D: Subtract exponents; the answer goes on top because 6 (on top) > 2.

40. A: A negative divided by a negative is a positive; the last zero must remain because $7 \times 80 = 560$.

Practice Test 1, Part II Answers

1. B: 2 hours 20 minutes $= 2\dfrac{1}{3}$ hours $= \dfrac{7}{3}$ hours ; $\dfrac{7}{3} \times 45 = 105$ miles.

2. B: We look at the number to the right of the tenths place; 4 is less than 5, so it and any numbers to the right of it are just dropped.

3. C: $\$38.50 \times 1.2 = \$46.20$.

4. C: $\dfrac{\text{red} + \text{white}}{\text{total}} = \dfrac{(3+8)}{15} = \dfrac{11}{15}$.

5. D: *Less than* means the first number gets subtracted.

6. A: The differences between the numbers increase by 2.

7. C: A diameter is a line segment through the center from one part of the circle to the other.

8. A: A radius is a line segment from the center to the edge of the circle.

9. D: A chord is a line segment from one side of the circle to the other; a diameter is the largest chord.

10. B: A secant is a line cutting the circle in two places.

11. C: A chord is a line segment from one side of the circle to the other.

12. C: $r = 8$; $(2)(3.14)(8) = 50.24$.

13. B: $2x > -4y + 8$, or $x > -2y + 4$.

14. D: 15 hours $= 15 \times 60 = 900$ minutes; $11,160,000 \times 900 = 1.116 \times 10^7 \times 9 \times 10^2 \approx 10^1 \times 10^9 = 10^{10}$.

15. C: $28 \div \dfrac{5}{4} = 28 \times \dfrac{4}{5} = \dfrac{112}{5} = 22\dfrac{2}{5}$, or 22 full pieces.

16. B: $20 = 2000(.04)t$; $80t = 20$; $t = 20/80 = \dfrac{1}{4}$ year $= 3$ months.

17. D: In order, we have 80, 80, 80, 80, 80, 85, 85, 85, 90, 90, 90, 90, 95, 95, 100, and 100. It is an even number of grades; the middle two are 85 and 90. The mean of these two is

$\dfrac{(85 + 90)}{2} = 87.5$, the median.

18. A: The mode is the most common number.

19. C: $\dfrac{(5 \times 80) + (4 \times 90) + (3 \times 85) + (2 \times 100) + (2 \times 95)}{16} = \dfrac{1405}{16} = 87.8$.

20. D: $100 - 80 = 20$.

21. C: $3x + 4x = 84$; $7x = 84$; $x = 12$; $4x = 4(12) = 48$.

22. B

23. D: For December, the average daily temperature of city B is 60° and the average daily temperature of city A is approximately 40°; their difference is 20°. The corresponding difference in temperatures between these two cities in January, February, and August are 16°, 14°, and 10°, respectively.

24. C: They are about the same in May and October. So we are interested in the months of June (with a temperature difference of 4°), July (with a temperature difference of 8°), August (with a temperature difference of 12°), and September (with a temperature difference of 10°), so the average is $\dfrac{4+8+12+10}{4} = 8.5$.

25. C: $\dfrac{\text{increase (city } B - \text{city } A)}{\text{city } A} = \dfrac{50-34}{34} = \dfrac{16}{34} = \dfrac{8}{17} \approx 47\%$.

26. C: Decrease $= \dfrac{\text{about } 60-40}{\text{city } B} = \dfrac{20}{60} = \dfrac{1}{3} = 33\frac{1}{3}\%$.

27. C: The temperature over 60 = 98 − 60 = 38; The number of 5° increases $= \dfrac{38}{5} \approx 7.6$; so the SPF increase is 7.6 × 3 = 22.8 ≈ 23. Therefore, the SPF needed is 23 + 15 = 38 SPF.

28. D: $5^2 + 12^2 = 13^2$, or 25 + 144 = 169. For a right triangle, $c^2 = a^2 + b^2$, where c is the longest side. The only choice for which this is true is D.

29. B: $2x = -6, x = -3$.

30. C: $\dfrac{2}{5}(400) = 160$ black; $\dfrac{1}{4}(160) = 40$ replaced with silver; 160 − 40 = 120 remain black.

31. B

32. C: $\left(\dfrac{7+3}{2}, \dfrac{5+2}{2}\right) = (5, 3.5)$.

33. C: $\triangle XYZ$ is a 3−4−5 Pythagorean triple, again! $XZ = 5$.

34. A: Area $= \dfrac{1}{2}bh = \dfrac{1}{2}(XY \times YZ) = \dfrac{1}{2}(4)(3) = 6$.

35. B: $\dfrac{2}{\frac{1}{3}} = \dfrac{7}{x}$; $2x = \dfrac{7}{3}$; so $x = \dfrac{7}{6}$, or $1\frac{1}{6}$.

36. A: $r = 3$; A = 3.14 × 3 × 3 = 28.26.

37. A: C = 2 × 3.14 × 3 = 18.84.

38. B: $\dfrac{1}{3}(3.14) \times 3 \times 3 \times 4 = 37.68$.

39. A: Again, $\triangle ABE$ is a $3-4-5$ Pythagorean triple, with $BE = 5$.

40. B: "At least" means "greater than or equal to."

41. C: $12 \times 7 \times 8 = 672$ (remember that 1 foot = 12 inches).

42. A: Multiply by 2 to get $3x + 20 = 44$. Then $3x = 24$, $x = 8$.

43. B: There were $30 - 19 = 11$ males; for the children, $16 - 10$ female children = 6 male children. So 11 males − 6 male children = 5 male adults.

44. D: There are 32 ounces in a quart. $\frac{222}{32} = 6\frac{30}{32}$.

45. A: $\$33 - \frac{1}{4}(33) = \$33.00 - \$8.25 = \$24.75$.

46. C: Base = 12 and height = 8; $A = \frac{1}{2}bh = \frac{1}{2}(12)(8) = 48$.

47. B: Like in Washington, D.C.

48. B: $\frac{\$30.80}{1.4} = \$22$; remember that $100\% + 40\% = 1.4$ as a decimal.

49. B: Only 3 divides evenly into all of the numbers.

50. B: $45 - 20 + 1$; let's say you read from the top of page 3 to page 10; you don't read 7 pages, you read 8; count them.

CHAPTER 11: *Practice Test 2*

"*Be patient, more practice may be needed for success.*"

Part I: Mathematics Computation

Note *No calculator permitted.*

1. $3.11 - 1.33 =$

   A 2.88   D 1.78

   B 2.78   E None of these

   C 1.88

2. $|4| - |-4| =$

   A 8   D 28

   B 4   E None of these

   C 0

3. $1 - 4^2 + 5 =$

   A -2 D -20

   B 14   E None of these

   C -10

4. $^-6 - {}^-2 =$

   A -12 D 12

   B -8 E None of these

   C -4

5. $\dfrac{24}{-12}$

        A 12   **D** −12

        B 2   **E** None of these

        C −2

6. $(.004)(.02) =$

        A .0008   **D** .0000008

        B .00008   **E** None of these

        C .000008

7. 87650 in scientific notation is

        A 876.5×10^2 **D** $.8765 \times 10^5$

        B 87.65×10^3 **E** None of these

        C 8.765×10^4

8. $\dfrac{5}{6} + \dfrac{5}{6} =$

        A $\dfrac{10}{12}$ **D** $\dfrac{25}{36}$

        B $\dfrac{5}{3}$ **E** None of these

        C $\dfrac{25}{6}$

9. $(3^2 - 1^2)^2 =$

        A 16   **D** 128

        B 32   **E** None of these

        C 64

10. $^-3 - 4 - {}^-9 =$

        A −16   **D** 108

        B −2   **E** None of these

        C 2

11. $\dfrac{.00014}{.02} =$

    A 7

    B .7

    C .07

    D .007

    E None of these

12. 9 is ___% of 4?

    A $44\dfrac{4}{9}\%$

    B 36%

    C $2\dfrac{1}{4}\%$

    D 225%

    E None of these

13. $\left(\dfrac{2}{3}\right)^2 =$

    A $\dfrac{4}{6}$

    B $\dfrac{4}{9}$

    C $\dfrac{4}{3}$

    D $\dfrac{2}{9}$

    E None of these

14. $10\dfrac{1}{3} - 5\dfrac{1}{2} =$

    A $5\dfrac{5}{6}$

    B $5\dfrac{1}{6}$

    C $4\dfrac{5}{6}$

    D $4\dfrac{1}{6}$

    E None of these

15. 12% of ___ = 24.

    A 2

    B 2.88

    C 200

    D 288

    E None of these

16. $5(5x^2 - 6) =$

    A $5x^2 - 6$ **D** $25x^2 - 30$

    B $25x^2 - 6$ **E** None of these

    C $25x^2 - 11$

17. 120% of 30 =

    A 24   **D** 48

    B 32   **E** None of these

    C 40

18. $(7 - 3^2)(7 + 3^2) =$

    A -200 **D** 200

    B -32 **E** None of these

    C 32

19. $\left(\dfrac{3}{4}\right)\left(\dfrac{9}{11}\right) =$

    A $\dfrac{4}{5}$ **D** $\dfrac{11}{12}$

    B $\dfrac{9}{5}$ **E** None of these

    C $\dfrac{27}{44}$

20. $\sqrt{400}$

    A 200   **D** 20

    B 100   **E** None of these

    C 50

21. $\dfrac{x}{6} = 6;\ x =$

    A 0   **D** 36

    B 1   **E** None of these

    C 12

22. What is 20% of 20?

    A 1   D 400

    B 4   E None of these

    C 5

23. $2\frac{1}{2} \times 2\frac{1}{2} =$

    A $4\frac{1}{4}$ D $6\frac{1}{2}$

    B 5   E None of these

    C $6\frac{1}{4}$

24. $0 - 3 =$

    A 3   D -3

    B 0   E None of these

    C -2

25. $(^{-}3)^3 - 3$

    A -12 D -30

    B -24 E None of these

    C -27

26. $x - 7 = 7; x =$

    A 0   D 47

    B 1   E None of these

    C 14

27. $\frac{3}{5} \div \frac{1}{4} =$

    A $\frac{4}{9}$ D $\frac{20}{3}$

    B $\frac{12}{5}$ E None of these

    E $\frac{3}{20}$

28. $4x + 5 + 7x + 8 =$

        A $24x$ **D** $24x^2$

        B $11x + 13$ **E** None of these

        C $11x + 40$

29. $1^2 + 2^2 + 3^2 + 4^2 =$

        A 100 **D** 20

        B 30 **E** None of these

        C 29

30. $10^{-2} \times 10^{-3} =$

        A $.01$ **D** $.000001$

        B $.001$ **E** None of these

        C $.00001$

31. $5 + \dfrac{3}{2} =$

        A $5\dfrac{1}{2}$ **D** $8\dfrac{1}{2}$

        B $6\dfrac{1}{2}$ **E** None of these

        C $7\dfrac{1}{2}$

32. $\sqrt{5^2 - 4^2} =$

        A 1 **D** 4

        B 2 **E** None of these

        C 3

33. $\dfrac{x^4}{x^{12}} =$

        A x^{48} **D** $\dfrac{1}{x^{48}}$

        B x^8 **E** None of these

        C $\dfrac{1}{x^8}$

34. $\dfrac{-770}{11}$

    A -659 **D** 1870

    B -70 **E** None of these

    C 70

35. $8 + 20 \div 2 - 1 =$

    A 17   **D** -160

    B 13   **E** None of these

    C 28

36. $\left(\dfrac{a}{b}\right)\left(\dfrac{c}{d}\right) =$

    A $\dfrac{(a+c)}{(b+d)}$ **D** $\dfrac{bd}{ac}$

    B $\dfrac{ad}{bc}$ **E** None of these

    C $\dfrac{ac}{bd}$

37. $4 + 0 + 0(4) + \dfrac{0}{4} =$

    A 0   **D** 12

    B 4   **E** None of these

    C 8

38. 12.4% of ___ is 12.4?

    A 0   **D** 100

    B 1   **E** None of these

    C 10

39. $\dfrac{74}{5}$ as a mixed number is

    A $9\dfrac{2}{5}$ **D** $18\dfrac{2}{5}$

    B 14   **E** None of these

    C $14\dfrac{4}{5}$

40. $32 + 3.2 + .32 =$

        A 96   **D** 35.52

        B 9.6   **E** None of these

        C .96

Part II: Applied Mathematics

Note *Calculators are permitted.*

1. Ida dove into the water from a height of 12 feet to a depth of 25 feet. Her change in height in feet was

        A 37 feet   **C** -13 feet

        B 13 feet   **D** -37 feet

2. Jo took her friends out to dinner. If the bill was \$97.43 after a 20% tip, how much did the dinner cost?

        A \$81.19   **C** \$87.11

        B \$83.37   **D** \$116.92

3. Ken drove 9 miles north and 12 miles east. How far from home was he in miles?

        A 15   **C** 19

        B 17   **D** 21

4,   In Springfield, 400 people voted for an increase in taxes and 700 voted against it. A person was chosen at random. The probability that the person voted for the increase is

        A $\dfrac{4}{7}$ **C** $\dfrac{7}{4}$

        B $\dfrac{4}{11}$ **D** $\dfrac{7}{11}$

5. Len earned E dollars a month. R dollars were for rent and U dollars were for utilities. P dollars were left for the rest of his expenses. What was P?

        A $P = E - (R - U)$ **C** $P = E + A + U$

        B $P = E - A + U$ **D** $P = E - R - U$

For problems 6–13, use the following chart.

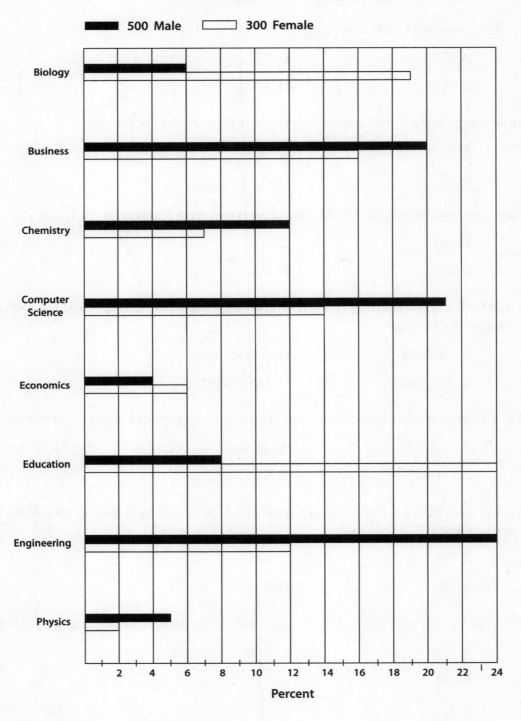

**Percent of male and female faculty population
at college in math-related fields**

6. How many men teach biology?

    A 6   **C** 30

    B 15   **D** 57

7. How many women teach chemistry?

    A 7   **C** 21

    B 12   **D** 60

8. In how many fields is the female faculty more than 7% of the faculty?

    A 1   **C** 3

    B 2   **D** 4

9. How many more of the men than the women faculty are in computer science?

    A 40   **C** 63

    B 57   **D** 77

10. In what field are the number of men on the faculty approximately equal to the number of women on the faculty?

    A Biology   **C** Economics

    B Business   **D** Education

11. If 450 students are in physics, the ratio of students to physics faculty is closest to

    A 9 to 1   **C** 15 to 1

    B 12 to 1   **D** 18 to 1

12. If the male numbers in the biology department increased by 80%, the total male biology faculty would be

    A 24   **C** 44

    B 30   **D** 54

13. If the male faculty in engineering were decreased by 10%, how many would there be?

    A 12   **C** 108

    B 24   **D** 120

14. In the sequence 1, −3, 5, −7, ..., the product of the next two terms is

    A −99   C 2

    B −2   D 99

15. May buys 3 loaves of bread at $1.99 a loaf. If she has up to $40 to spend, write the expression for how much, F, she has left.

    A $F \leq \$40 + 3 \times \$1.99$

    B $F \geq \$40 + 3 \times \$1.99$

    C $F \leq \$40 - 3 \times \$1.99$

    D $F \geq \$40 - 3 \times \$1.99$

16. A $420 skateboard is discounted 20%. With 5% sales tax, Ned pays

    A $339.36   C $362.21

    B $352.80   D $525.00

17. Any line segment from one part of a circle to another is a

    A Tangent   C Radius

    B Secant   D Chord

18. A line segment from one corner of a square through the center to the opposite corner is called a

    A Side   C Base

    B Leg   D Diagonal

19. The area of a trapezoid is $A = \frac{1}{2}h(b_1 + b_2)$, where h = height, and b_1 and b_2 are the two bases. If the height of a trapezoid is 40 feet and the bases are 17 and 11, the area is

    A 280   D 1120

    B 560   D 2240

20. The answer to $5x - 7 = 8x - 37$ is $x =$

    A $-\dfrac{44}{13}$ C +10

    B −10   D $+\dfrac{44}{13}$

For problems 21–25, use the following data: In one week, the noon temperatures (Monday though Sunday) were 69°, 71°, 71°, 67°, 72°, 75°, 79°.

21. The mean temperature at noon was

        A 69°   C 72°

        B 71°   D 77°

22. The mode temperature at noon was

        A 69°   C 72°

        B 71°   D 77°

23. The median temperature at noon was

        A 69°   C 72°

        B 71°   D 77°

24. The mean weekend temperature at noon was exactly

        A 75°   C 78°

        B 77°   D 154 °

25. The range is the highest minus the lowest. The range for this week was

        A 2°   C 12°

        B 10°   D 22°

26. At 2:15 Opie started his trip by plane, reaching his destination at 4:45. The plane traveled 1100 miles. The average plane speed was

        A $366\frac{2}{3}$ mph   C 500 mph

        B 440 mph   D 550 mph

27. The equation for "six less than three times a number is the same as 4 less eight times the same number" can be written

        A $3x - 6 = 8x - 4$ C $6 - 3x = 8x - 4$

        B $3x - 6 = 4 - 8x$ D $6 - 3x = 4 - 8x$

28. Which equation is equivalent to $7y - 14x = 35$?

        A $y = -2x - 5$ C $y = -2x + 5$

        B $y = 2x - 5$ D $y = 2x + 5$

29. Sound travels approximately 1100 feet per second. In $1\frac{1}{2}$ minutes, sound travels approximately how many feet?

    A 10^3 **C** 10^5

    B 10^4 **D** 10^6

For problems 30–37, use the two figures graphed below.

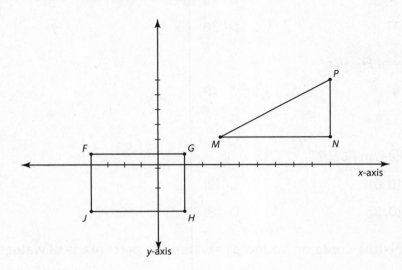

30. The coordinates of point *F* are

    A (4, 1)   **C** (−4, 1)

    B (4, 21)   **D** (−4, −1)

31. The area of triangle *MNP* is

    A 7   **C** 17

    B 12   **D** 24

32. The length of *MP* is approximately

    A 6   **C** 9

    B 7   **D** 10

33. The perimeter of triangle *MNP* is approximately

    A 11   **C** 15

    B 13   **D** 17

34. Figure *FGHJ* is a

    A Rectangle   **C** Rhombus
    B Square   **D** Trapezoid

35. The area of *FGHJ* is

    A 9   **C** 18
    B 12   **D** 36

36. The perimeter of *FGHJ* is

    A 9   **C** 18
    B 12   **D** 36

37. Which point lies on *FGHJ*?

    A (0, 0)   **C** (0, −2)
    B (0, 3)   **D** (3, 0)

38. An 8-ounce mixture contains 3 ounces of water. The percentage of water in the mixture is

    A 25   **C** 37.5
    B $33\frac{1}{3}$ **D** $42\frac{1}{6}$

39. The part of a line that is on one side of a point is a

    A Line segment   **C** Secant
    B Tangent   **D** Ray

40. A cube that is 5 cm on each edge has a volume in cubic centimeters of

    A 15   **C** 150
    B 125   **C** 625

41. 654 millimeters equals how many meters?

    A 65.4   **C** 0.654
    B 6.54   **D** 0.0654

42. If point (x, y) is in the second quadrant, then

   A $x > 0, y > 0$ **C** $x < 0, y < 0$

   B $x > 0, y < 0$ **D** $x < 0, y > 0$

43. Pat had a choice of 4 sandwiches, 4 desserts, and 2 drinks. If Pat could choose one of each, the total number of different meals from which he can choose is

   A 10   **C** 32

   B 16   **D** 1024

44. Quincy's stock holdings dropped from $116 to $96. The percentage loss was about

   A 10   **C** 17

   B 14   **D** 20

45. Which inequality will make $9x - 2 > 43$ true?

   A $x \geq 45$ **C** $x \geq 5$

   B $x > 45$ **D** $x > 5$

46. In the sequence 6, 1, -5, -12, ____, -29, -39, the missing number is

   A -18 **C** -20

   B -19 **D** -21

47. 45 written as the product of prime factors is

   A 3(5)   **C** 3(15)

   B 9(5)   **D** (3)(3)(5)

48. Two-thirds of women like Brand A, and $\frac{2}{3}$ of those women also like Brand B. What fraction of women like Brand A and do not like Brand B?

   A $\frac{2}{9}$ **C** $\frac{4}{9}$

   B $\frac{1}{3}$ **D** $\frac{2}{3}$

49. A half ton equals how many ounces?

   A 160   **C** 16,000

   B 1600   **D** 160,000

50. $4\frac{1}{2}$ yards = _____ inches?

    A 13.5   C 144

    B 27   D 162

Practice Test 2, Part I Answers

1. D: Align the decimals.

2. C: $4 - 4 = 0$; remember that $|-4| = 4$.

3. C: $1 - 16 + 5 = -10$.

4. C: $-6 + 2 = -4$.

5. C: A positive divided by a negative is negative.

6. B: The number of decimal places in the answer is the sum of the decimal places in the multipliers, $3 + 3 = 5$, so it is .00008.

7. C: Remember that the number part has only one digit before the decimal point.

8. B: $\frac{10}{6} = \frac{5}{3}$.

9. C: $8^2 = 64$.

10. C: $-3 + (-4) + 9 = 2$

11. D: $\frac{.014}{2} = .007$. Make sure the decimal point in the numerator is moved the same number of places that the denominator must be moved to become a whole number.

12. D: $\frac{9}{4} \times 100\% = 225\%$.

13. B: $\left(\frac{2}{3}\right) \times \left(\frac{2}{3}\right)$; then multiply the tops and the bottoms separately.

14. C: $10\frac{2}{6} - 5\frac{3}{6} = 9\frac{8}{6} - 5\frac{3}{6} = 4\frac{5}{6}$.

15. C: $\frac{24}{.12} = \frac{2400}{12} = 200$.

16. D: Use the distributive property of multiplication over subtraction.

17. E: $1.2 \times 30 = 36$.

18. B: $(-2)(16) = -32$.

19. C: Multiply the tops and multiply the bottoms; nothing cancels here.

20. D: $20^2 = 400$.

21. D: Multiply each side by 6.

22. B: $(.2)(20) = 4$.

23. C: $\dfrac{5}{2} \times \dfrac{5}{2} = \dfrac{25}{4} = 6\dfrac{1}{4}$.

24. D: $0 + (-3) = -3$.

25. D: $-27 - 3 = -30$.

26. C: Add 7 to each side.

27. B: $\dfrac{3}{5} \times \dfrac{4}{1} = \dfrac{12}{5}$.

28. B: Add like terms only.

29. B: $1 + 4 + 9 + 16 = 30$.

30. C: Add exponents: $10^{-2} \times 10^{-3} = 10^{-5}$ (move decimal point 5 places to the left of 1: .00001).

31. B: $5 + 1\dfrac{1}{2} = 6\dfrac{1}{2}$.

32. C: $\sqrt{25 - 16} = \sqrt{9} = 3$.

33. C: Subtract exponents; the answer is in the bottom because $4 < 12$.

34. B: A negative divided by a positive is negative.

35. A: Do the division first: $8 + 10 - 1 = 17$.

36. C: Multiply the tops and multiply the bottoms.

37. B: $4 + 0 + 0 + 0 = 4$.

38. D: Percent means divided by 100, so to keep the same number, you must multiply by 100.

39. C: 5 into 74 = 14 plus remainder 4 $\left(\dfrac{4}{5}\right)$, so it is $14\dfrac{4}{5}$.

40. D: Line up the decimal points.

Practice Test 2, Part II Answers

1. D: 12 feet above the water + 25 feet underwater.

2. A: $\dfrac{\$97.43}{1.2} = 81.19$ (remember that 100% + 20% tip = 1.2 as a decimal).

3. A: This is a 9−12−15 right triangle, $\sqrt{9^2 + 12^2} = \sqrt{225} = 15$

4. B: $\dfrac{400}{(400 + 700)} = \dfrac{400}{1100} = \dfrac{4}{11}$.

5. D: $P = E − (R + U) = E − R − U$.

6. C: .06(500) = 30.

7. C: .07(300) = 21.

8. B: The faculty has 800 members. 7% of 800 is 56. Education and biology are the only departments with more than 56 female members (or more than 18.7% of the females).

9. C: 21% of 500 is 105; 14% of 300 is 42; 105 − 42 = 63.

10. C: The percentage of women must be close to $\dfrac{5}{3} \times$ the percentage of men. This is true only for economics.

11. C: 5% of 500 = 25 male faculty, and 2% of 300 = 6 female faculty. The total faculty is 31. $\dfrac{450}{31} \approx \dfrac{15}{1}$.

12. D: 6% of 500 = 30. Then 30 + .8(30) = 30 + 24 = 54.

13. C: .24(500) − .24(500)(.10) = 120 − 12 = 108.

14. A: 9(−11) = −99.

15. C: She has "up to," meaning "less than or equal to."

16. B: 420(.8)(1.05) = 352.80.

17. D: This is the definition of *chord*.

18. D: This is the definition of a diagonal of a square.

19. B: $\frac{1}{2}(40)(17 + 11) = 560$.

20. C: $-3x = -30$; divide by -3 on both sides.

21. C: Add them up and divide by 7.

22. B: The most common number.

23. B: The middle when the temperatures are arranged lowest to highest.

24. B: $\frac{(75 + 79)}{2} = 77$.

25. C: $79 - 67 = 12$.

26. B: $\frac{1100 \text{ miles}}{2.5 \text{ hours}} = 440$ mph.

27. B: "Less than" reverses the numbers; "less" does not; you must read every word carefully.

28. D: Divide each term by 7.

29. C: $1\frac{1}{2}$ minutes = 90 seconds, so $1100 \times 90 = 99000 \approx 10^5$, or $1.1 \times 10^3 \times 9 \times 10^1 \approx 10^5$.

30. C

31. B: $A = \frac{1}{2}bh = \frac{1}{2}(6)(4) = 12$.

32. B: This is a right triangle, so $MP = \sqrt{6^2 + 4^2} = \sqrt{52} \approx 7$.

33. D: $4 + 6 + 7 = 17$.

34. A

35. C: $A = bh = 6 \times 3 = 18$.

36. C: $6 + 6 + 3 + 3 = 18$.

37. C

38. C: $\frac{3}{8} = 37\frac{1}{2}\%$.

39. D: This is the definition of *ray*.

40. B: $5^3 = 125$; remember, cubing comes from a cube (and squaring comes from a square).

41. C: Each millimeter is $\frac{1}{1000}$ of a meter, so 654 millimeters $= \frac{654}{1000}$ meters $= 0.654$ meters.

42. D

43. C: $(4)(4)(2) = 32$.

44. C: $\frac{(116 - 96)}{116} \times 100\% = \frac{20}{116} \times 100\% = 17.2\%$.

45. D: Add 2 to each side: $9x > 45$; then divide by 9.

46. C: Each term decreases by one more than the previous decrease.

47. D: 9 is not prime; it is (3)(3).

48. A: $\left(\frac{2}{3}\right)\left(\frac{2}{3}\right) = \frac{4}{9}$ of the women like both; so $\frac{2}{3} - \frac{4}{9} = \frac{6}{9} - \frac{4}{9} = \frac{2}{9}$ of the women like Brand A, but do not like Brand B.

49. C: 1000 pounds $\times \frac{16 \text{ ounces}}{1 \text{ pound}} = 16,000$ ounces.

50. D: 4.5 yards $\times \frac{36 \text{ inches}}{1 \text{ yard}} = 162$ inches.

"*Be patient, more practice may be needed for success.*"

Part I: Mathematics Computation

Note *No calculator permitted.*

1. 20% of 50 − 50% of 20 =

    A 0   **D** 40

    B 10   **E** None of these

    C 20

2. .4201 − .1204 =

    A .2997   **D** .2003

    B .3997   **E** None of these

    C .3003

3. $x + 14 = 12; x =$

    A 2   **D** −168

    B −2   **E** None of these

    C 26

4. The median of 5, 5, 7, 8, 15 is

    A 5   **D** 8

    B 6   **E** None of these

    C 7

5. The mode of 5, 5, 7, 8, 15 is

  A 5   **D** 8

  B 6   **E** None of these

  C 7

6. The mean of 5, 5, 7, 8, 15 is

  A 5   **D** 8

  B 6   **E** None of these

  C 7

7. $\frac{3}{4} + \frac{3}{4} + \frac{3}{4} =$

  A $\frac{9}{4}$ **D** $3\frac{3}{4}$

  B $\frac{9}{64}$ **E** None of these

  C $\frac{27}{64}$

8. $10^{-3} =$

  A $\frac{1}{1000}$ **D** -30

  B $\frac{3}{1000}$ **E** None of these

  C $\frac{1}{30}$

9. $2x - 3 = 17; x =$

  A 7   **D** 13

  B 9   **E** None of these

  C 10

10. $-|-3| - |3| =$

  A -6 **D** 3

  B -3 **E** None of these

  C 0

11. $^-6 - 4 + {}^-2 =$

    A -12 **D** 0

    B -8 **E** None of these

    C -4

12. $\left(\dfrac{3}{10}\right) \times \left(\dfrac{10}{9}\right) =$

    A $\dfrac{1}{3}$ **D** 9

    B 1 **E** None of these

    C 3

13. $\left(\dfrac{3}{5}\right)\left(\dfrac{5}{3}\right) =$

    A 0 **D** $\dfrac{9}{25}$

    B 1 **E** None of these

    C $\dfrac{25}{9}$

14. $3.45 \times 10^4 =$

    A 345000 **D** 345000000

    B 3450000 **E** None of these

    C 34500000

15. $2^3 \times 3^2 =$

    A 17 **D** 46656

    B 72 **E** None of these

    C 7776

16. $7 - (7 \div 7) - 7 =$

    A -1 **D** 14

    B 0 **E** None of these

    C 1

17. ___% of 8 is 6.

      A 48　　　　　　　　**D** $233\frac{1}{3}$

      B 75　　　　　　　　**E** None of these

      C $133\frac{1}{3}$

18. $5x + 2x = -35; x =$

      A −5　　　　　　　　**D** 5

      B −3.5　　　　　　　**E** None of these

      C 3.5

19. $10^6 10^7 =$

      A 10^{13}　　　　　　　**D** 100^{42}

      B 10^{42}　　　　　　　**E** None of these

      C 100^{13}

20. $2x + 7 - 5x - 3 =$

      A $210x$　　　　　　　**D** $10x - 4$

      B $210x^2$　　　　　　　**E** None of these

      C $10x + 4$

21. $10 - 3^2 - 1 =$

      A 0　　　　　　　　**D** 49

      B 3　　　　　　　　**E** None of these

      C 48

22. $3\frac{2}{3} + 5\frac{1}{3} =$

      A 8　　　　　　　　**D** 16

      B 9　　　　　　　　**E** None of these

      C $15\frac{2}{8}$

23. $\frac{4}{7} \div \frac{7}{4} =$

    A 0   **D** $\frac{49}{16}$

    B 1   **E** None of these

    C $\frac{16}{49}$

24. $\sqrt{\frac{4}{9}} =$

    A $\frac{2}{3}$ **D** 3

    B $\frac{3}{2}$ **E** None of these

    C 2

25. $11 - {}^{-}4 - 7 =$

    A 0   **D** 22

    B 7   **E** None of these

    C 8

26. $(2 - {}^{-}3)^2 =$

    A -1 **D** 36

    B 1   **E** None of these

    C 25

27. $\frac{a^4}{a} =$

    A 3   **D** a^4

    B 4   **E** None of these

    C a^3

28. 9 is 4.5% of

    A 40.5   **D** 405

    B 100   **E** None of these

    C 200

29. $3\frac{1}{2} \times \frac{2}{7} =$

    A $\frac{4}{49}$ D $\frac{49}{4}$

    B 1   E None of these

    C $3\frac{11}{14}$

30. $4(3x + 4) + 5 =$

    A $12x + 9$ D $12x + 36$

    B $12x + 21$ E None of these

    C $12x + 25$

31. Reduced, $\frac{24}{36} =$

    A $\frac{1}{2}$ D $\frac{7}{8}$

    B $\frac{2}{3}$ E None of these

    C $\frac{3}{4}$

32. .0000456 in scientific notation is

    A 0.456×10^{-4} D 456×10^{-7}

    B 4.56×10^{-5} E None of these

    C 45.6×10^{-6}

33. $1\frac{2}{3} - \frac{5}{3} =$

    A 0   D $\frac{100}{9}$

    B 1   E None of these

    C $\frac{10}{3}$

34. $(.000045)(200) =$

    A 0.0009   **D** 900

    B 0.009   **E** None of these

    C 0.09

35. 50% of .5 = ___

    A 0.25   **D** 250

    B 2.5   **E** None of these

    C 25

36. $2^6 =$

    A 12   **D** 64

    B 16   **E** None of these

    C 32

37. $(-1)^{101}$

    A -101 **D** 101

    B -1 **E** None of these

    C 1

38. $\sqrt{5 - 1^2} =$

    A 2   **D** 6

    B 4   **E** None of these

    C 5

39. $\dfrac{0}{6} + (0)(6) + 6 =$

    A 0   **D** 18

    B 6   **E** None of these

    C 12

40. $\dfrac{.007}{.07} =$

      A 0.001   **D** 1

      B 0.01   **E** None of these

      C 0.1

Part II: Applied Mathematics

Note *Calculators are permitted.*

1. Rob goes 2 hours at 60 miles per hour and 3 hours at 40 miles per hour. The total trip in miles is

      A 120   **C** 240

      B 180   **D** 14,400

2. A line touching the circle at only one point is a

      A Tangent   **C** Diameter

      B Secant   **D** Chord

3. $3x - 4 > 9$ is true if

      A $x > 2$ **C** $x > 13$

      B $x > -2$ **D** $x > \dfrac{13}{3}$

4. In a circuit, the total resistance, R, in ohms is given by the equation $\dfrac{1}{R} = \dfrac{1}{R_1} + \dfrac{1}{R_2}$. If $R_1 = 3$ and $R_2 = 6$, in ohms, $R =$

      A 1   **C** 12

      B 2   **D** 18

5. Sam uses $\dfrac{1}{4}$ of a 6-inch crayon in 1 day. In how many days is $1\dfrac{1}{2}$ inches remaining?

      A 5   **C** 18

      B 10   **D** 22

For problems 6–12, use the chart below.

Specialty-Store Larger Shoe Sizes

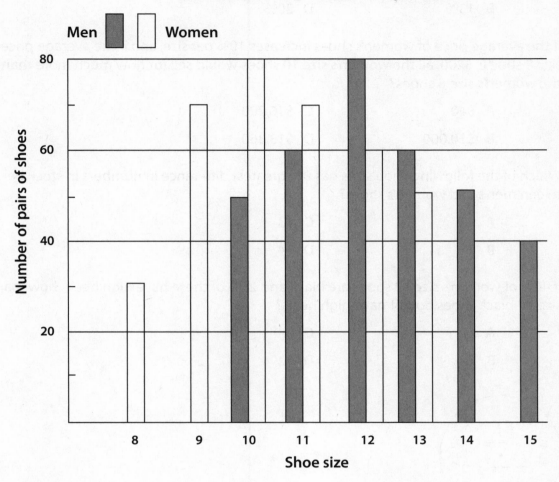

6. Which shoe size has the most shoes in the store?

   A 9   **C** 11

   B 10   **D** 12

7. Which shoe size has the least shoes in the store?

   A 8   **C** 14

   B 9   **D** 15

8. The difference in the number of pairs of shoes between men's size 12 and men's size 10 is

   A 0   **C** 20

   B 10   **D** 30

9. Of all the shoes in stock, the percentage of men's shoes greater than size 13 is about

    A 10%   **C** 16%

    B 13%   **D** 20%

10. If the average price of women's shoes increases 10% per size, and if the average price of a size 8 shoe is $200, all the women's size 10 shoes would sell for how much more than all the women's size 8 shoes?

    A $40   **C** $16,200

    B $10,000   **D** $13,360

11. Which of the following shoe sizes has the greatest difference in numbers in stock between men's and women's shoes?

    A 11   **C** 13

    B 12   **D** 14

12. If 40% of women's size 12 shoes are black and 25% of these have high heels, how many size 12 black shoes do not have high heels?

    A 18   **C** 28

    B 24   **D** 32

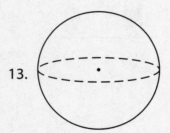

13.

A sphere has diameter 14. If $V = \left(\dfrac{4}{3}\right)\pi r^3$, and $\pi = \dfrac{22}{7}$, $V =$

    A 1000   **C** 11,498.7

    B 1437.3   **D** 27,777

14. If $x + a - b = c$, then $x =$

    A $c - b - a$ **C** $c + b - a$

    B $c - b + a$ **D** $c + b + a$

15. After a 30% discount, Tess pays $147 for a dress. The original price was

    A $102.90   **C** $210

    B $177   **D** $227

16. A 60-meter board is cut in the ratio of 3:4:5. The largest piece is

    A 15   **C** 25

    B 20   **D** 30

17. A 6-sided polygon is called a

    A Pentagon   **C** Nonagon

    B Hexagon   **D** Decagon

18. $4(2x - 5) = 8x - 20$ is an example of what property?

    A Commutative property of multiplication

    B Associative property of multiplication

    C Commutative property of subtraction

    D Distributive property of multiplication over subtraction

19. $(a + c) + 4 = 4 + (a + c)$ is an example of what property?

    A Commutative property of addition

    B Commutative property of multiplication

    C Associative property of addition

    D Associative property of multiplication

20. The supplement to a 20° angle is

    A 40°   **C** 80°

    B 70°   **D** 160°

21. If $\angle x$ is 50° and $\angle y$ is the vertical angle to $\angle x$, then $\angle y =$

    A 40°   **C** 60°

    B 50°   **D** 130°

For problems 22–26, use the following graph.

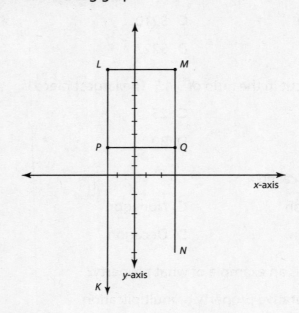

22. The coordinates of point *N* are

    A (3, 4)   **C** (−3, 4)

    B (3, −4)   **D** (−3, −4)

23. Which line segment lies on a ray?

    A *LP*   **C** *PQ*

    B *LM*   **D** All of the above

24. The perimeter of *LMQP* is

    A 20   **C** 24

    B 22   **D** 30

25. The area of *LMQP* is

    A 20   **C** 24

    B 22   **D** 30

26. The length of *KM* =

    A 13   **C** 16

    B 14   **D** 17

27. Simplified, $8x + 4y - 3x + y$ is

    A $9xy$ **C** $5y - 5x$

    B $5x + 5y$ **D** $5x + 4y$

28. The diameter of an atom is .000013 mm. In scientific notation, this is

    A 13×10^{-6} **C** 1.3×10^{-4}

    B 1.3×10^{-5} **D** 0.13×10^{-4}

29. 40% of 240 boxes are red and $\frac{1}{3}$ of these have stripes; how many are red and striped?

    A 32   **C** 80

    B 64   **D** 96

30. What number is missing from 1, 2, 4, 8, ___, 32?

    A 12   **C** 20

    B 16   **D** 28

31. If $3y - 6x > 9$, then

    A $y > 2x + 3$ **C** $y > -2x + 3$

    B $y > 2x - 3$ **D** $y > -2x - 3$

32. The area of a circle is $A = \pi r^2$, and $\pi = 3.14$; if $d = 200$, the area =

    A 31400   **C** 125600

    B 3140000   **D** 12560000

33. $\dfrac{x^6 y^6}{x^7 y^2} =$

    A xy^4 **C** $\dfrac{y^4}{x}$

    B $\dfrac{x}{y^4}$ **D** $\dfrac{1}{x^4 y}$

34. If $4x - 6x = 10$, $x =$

    A -5 **C** 1

    B -1 **D** 5

35. On a map, the scale is 1 inch = 20 miles. Then 145 miles is represented by ___ inches.

    A 7

    B $7\frac{1}{4}$

    C $7\frac{1}{2}$

    D 8

36. A $260 item is marked up 60%. Tom's cost is

    A $340

    B $400

    C $416

    D $438

37. If $x - m + n - ns = p$, then $x =$

    A $p - m + n - ns$

    B $p + m - n + ns$

    C pmn^2s

    D $p + m + n + ns$

38. The probability of selecting a vowel, a, e, i, o, u, from the alphabet is

    A $\frac{5}{21}$

    B $\frac{1}{21}$

    C $\frac{1}{26}$

    D $\frac{5}{26}$

For problems 39–41, use the following numbers: 5, 5, 5, 6, 7, 8, 9, 9, 10, 11.

39. The median is

    A 5

    B 7

    C 7.5

    D 8.5

40. The mode is

    A 5

    B 8.5

    C 9

    D 10

41. The mean is

    A 5

    B 7

    C 7.5

    D 8.5

42. $\sqrt{20^2 - 2^2}$ is closest to

    A 20

    B 19

    C 18

    D 16

43. 23 meters = ___ centimeters?

     A .0023   **C** 23,000

     B 2300   **D** 23,000,000

44. 1 yard 1 foot 1 inch = ____ inches.

     A 48   **C** 50

     B 49   **D** 85

45. A square is the same area as a rectangle. The base of the rectangle is $4\frac{1}{2}$ and the height is 8. The side of the square is

     A 5   **C** 7

     B 6   **D** $7\frac{1}{2}$

46. $5(2x + 4) + 3(6x - 7) =$

     A $28x + 1$ **C** $28x - 3$

     B $28x - 1$ **D** $180x - 3$

47.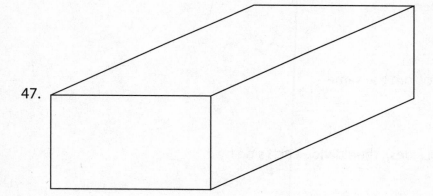

The volume in cubic millimeters of a box that is 3 centimeters by 5 millimeters by 7 centimeters is

     A 10.5   **C** 1050

     B 105   **D** 10,500

48. The diagonals of a rhombus are 12 and 5. Its area is

     A 13   **C** 60

     B 30   **D** 169

49. A $40 stock is sold for $46. The profit is

        A 10%   **C** 17.5%

        B 15%   **D** 20%

50. $\left(\dfrac{3}{4}\right) x = 48; x =$

        A 12   **C** 64

        B 36   **D** 192

Practice Test 3, Part I Answers

1. A: .20(50) − .50(20) = 10 − 10 = 0.

2. A: Align decimals before subtracting.

3. B: Subtract 14 from each side.

4. C: The middle number because they are already in order.

5. A: The most common number.

6. D: $\dfrac{(5+5+7+8+15)}{5} = 8.$

7. A: Add the tops; leave the bottom the same.

8. A: $\dfrac{1}{10^3} = \dfrac{1}{1000}.$

9. C: 2x = 20 (adding 3 to both sides); then divide each side by 2.

10. A: −3 + −3 = −6.

11. A: (−6) + (−4) + (−2) = −12.

12. A: The 10's cancel, and $\dfrac{3}{9} = \dfrac{1}{3}.$

13. B: $\dfrac{15}{15} = 1$, or cancel the 3's and 5's.

14. E: Because the exponent is +4, move the decimal point 4 places to the right: 34500.

15. B: 8 × 9 = 72.

16. A: $7 - 1 - 7 = -1$.

17. B: $\dfrac{6}{8} = \dfrac{3}{4} = 75\%$.

18. A: $7x = -35$; divide each side by 7.

19. A: Add the exponents; leave the base alone.

20. E: $2x - 5x = -3x$ and $7 - 3 = +4$; $-3x + 4$.

21. A: $10 - 9 - 1 = 0$.

22. B: $8\dfrac{1}{3} = 8 + 1 = 9$.

23. C: $\left(\dfrac{4}{7}\right)\left(\dfrac{4}{7}\right) = \dfrac{16}{49}$, multiplying the tops and bottoms together.

24. A: $\dfrac{\sqrt{4}}{\sqrt{9}} = \dfrac{2}{3}$.

25. C: $11 + 4 - 7 = 15 - 7 = 8$.

26. C: $5^2 = 25$.

27. C: $\dfrac{a^4}{a^1} = a^{4-1} = a^3$.

28. C: $\dfrac{9}{.045} = \dfrac{9000}{45} = 200$.

29. B: $\dfrac{7}{2} \times \dfrac{7}{2} = \dfrac{14}{14} = 1$.

30. B: $12x + 16 + 5 = 12x + 21$.

31. B: Divide top and bottom by 12, the greatest common factor.

32. B: The number before the decimal point must be between 1 and 9 (1 is possible also), and the power of 10 tells how many spaces the decimal point moved.

33. A: $\dfrac{5}{3} - \dfrac{5}{3} = 0$.

34. B: Multiply 200×45 and make sure the decimal point is six places from the right end.

35. A: $.5 \times .5 = .25$

36. D: $2 \times 2 \times 2 \times 2 \times 2 \times 2 = 64$.

37   B: If you multiply any number of ones, you get 1; an odd number of minus signs is minus.

38.   A: $\sqrt{4} = 2$.

39.   B: $0 + 0 + 6 = 6$.

40.   C: Multiply top and bottom by 1000 to clear decimal points: $\dfrac{7}{70} = 0.1$.

Practice Test 3, Part II Answers

1.   C: $2 \times 60 + 3 \times 40 = 120 + 120 = 240$.

2.   A: This is the definition of *tangent*.

3.   D: $3x > 13$, or $x > \dfrac{13}{3}$.

4.   B: $\dfrac{1}{R} = \dfrac{1}{3} + \dfrac{1}{6} = \dfrac{2}{6} + \dfrac{1}{6} = \dfrac{3}{6} = \dfrac{1}{2}$. Then $R = 2$.

5.   C: $6 - 1\dfrac{1}{2} = 4\dfrac{1}{2}$. Then $4\dfrac{1}{2} \div \dfrac{1}{4} = \left(\dfrac{9}{2}\right)\left(\dfrac{4}{1}\right) = 18$

6.   D: Be sure to look at both men's and women's shoes.

7.   A

8.   D: $80 - 50 = 30$.

9.   B: All shoes total $30 + 70 + 50 + 80 + 60 + 70 + 80 + 60 + 60 + 50 + 50 + 40 = 700$.

   $\dfrac{90}{700} \times 100\% \approx 13\%$.

10.   D: Size 8 costs $200; $200 \times 30 = $6,000$; Size 9 costs $200 + .10(200) = 220; Size 10 costs $220 + .10(220) = 242; $242 \times 80 = $19,360$; $19,360 - $6,000 = $13,360$.

11.   D: For size 14, $50 - 0 = 50$.

12.   A: $60 \times .4 = 24$. If 25% have high heels, then 75% do not have high heels, so $24 \times .75 = 18$.

13.   B: $r = 7$. $V = \left(\dfrac{4}{3}\right)\left(\dfrac{22}{7}\right)(343) = 1437.3$

14.   C: When you change sides, you switch signs.

15.   C: $147 is thus 70% of the original price, so $\dfrac{\$147}{.7} = \$210$.

16. C: $3x + 4x + 5x = 60$; $12x = 60$; $x = 5$. The largest piece is $5x = 25$.

17. B: This is the definition of *hexagon*.

18. D

19. A: Only the order is changed.

20. D: $180 - 20 = 160$.

21. B: Vertical angles are the same.

22. B

23. A

24. B: $6 + 5 + 6 + 5 = 22$.

25. D: $(5)(6) = 30$.

26. A: It is the longest side of a $5-12-13$ Pythagorean triple.

27. B: $8x - 3x + 4y + 1y = 5x + 5y$.

28. B: The decimal point must be moved 5 places to the right to get 1.3. Even though 13×10^{-6} and 0.13×10^{-4} are equivalent, 13 and 0.13 are not between 1 and 10, so it is not in scientific notation.

29. A: $.4 \times 240 \times \dfrac{1}{3} = 32$.

30. B: Each number is double the previous number.

31. A: $3y > 6x + 9$; then divide everything by 3.

32. A: If the diameter is 200, $r = 100$; so $3.14 \times 100 \times 100 = 31400$.

33. C: Subtract exponents when you divide; x^{-1} is the same as $\dfrac{1}{x}$.

34. A: $-2x = 10$; divide each side by -2.

35. B: The proportion is $\dfrac{20}{1} = \dfrac{145}{x}$; $20x = 145$; $x = \dfrac{145}{20} = 7\dfrac{1}{4}$.

36. C: $\$260 + \$260 \times .6 = \$260 + \$156 = \$416$.

37. B: When the terms switch sides, they change sign.

38. D: $\dfrac{5 \text{ vowels}}{26 \text{ letters}}$

39. C: The median is the middle number; if there are two middle numbers, it is their average,

$\dfrac{(7+8)}{2} = 7.5$.

40. A: The most common number.

41. C: $\dfrac{75}{10} = 7.5$.

42. A: $\sqrt{400 - 4} = \sqrt{396} \approx 19.9$, closest to 20.

43. B: When changing from larger to smaller, multiply, in this case by 100 because 1 meter = 100 centimeters.

44. B: $36 + 12 + 1 = 49$.

45. B: $A = 4.5 \times 8 = 36 = s^2; s = \sqrt{36} = 6$.

46. B: $10x + 20 + 18x - 21 = 10x + 18x + 20 - 21 = 28x - 1$.

47. D: Change all dimensions to millimeters (1 centimeter = 10 millimeters); $30 \times 5 \times 70 = 10{,}500$.

48. B: For a rhombus, $A = \dfrac{1}{2}$ (the product of the diagonals) $= \left(\dfrac{1}{2}\right)(5)(12) = 30$.

49. B: Percentage profit $= \dfrac{\text{profit}}{\text{original price}} \times 100\% = \dfrac{6}{40} \times 100\% = 15\%$.

50. C: Multiply by 4; $3x = 192$; then divide by 3; $x = 64$.

Part I: Mathematics Computation

Note *No calculator permitted.*

1. .222 + 3.33 + 44.4 =

    A 0.999   **D** 49.992

    B 99.45   **E** None of these

    C 47.952

2. $\dfrac{1}{2} + \dfrac{1}{3} + \dfrac{1}{6} =$

    A $\dfrac{1}{18}$ **D** 2

    B $\dfrac{3}{11}$ **E** None of these

    C 1

3. $\sqrt{144} =$

    A 72   **D** 12

    B 36   **E** None of these

    C 24

4. $4x = -32; x =$

    A −128   **D** −8

    B −62   **E** None of these

    C −36

5. 40% of ___ = 120.

    A 30   D 480

    B 48   E None of these

    C 300

6. $\dfrac{-24}{24}$

    A −36   D 0

    B −12   E None of these

    C −1

7. $2 - 6^2 - 4 =$

    A −38   D 12

    B −14   E None of these

    C 0

8. $|6 - 4| - |4 - 6| =$

    A −4   D 20

    B 0   E None of these

    C 4

9. $4 \times 10^{-1} =$

    A $-\dfrac{2}{5}$ D $\dfrac{2}{5}$

    B $\dfrac{1}{40}$ E None of these

    C $\dfrac{1}{4}$

10. The mode of 3, 4, 4, 3, 4, 12 is

    A 3   D 6

    B 3.5   E None of these

    C 4

11. The median of 3, 4, 4, 3, 4, 12 is

    A 3   **D** 6

    B 3.5   **E** None of these

    C 4

12. The mean of 3, 4, 4, 3, 4, 12 is

    A 3   **D** 6

    B 3.5   **E** None of these

    C 4

13. $\dfrac{3}{4} \times \dfrac{9}{11} =$

    A $\dfrac{27}{44}$ **D** $\dfrac{36}{33}$

    B $\dfrac{33}{36}$ **E** None of these

    C 1

14. $\dfrac{.141}{3} =$

    A .47   **D** 4.23

    B 4.7   **E** None of these

    C 47

15. $10^2 - 10 =$

    A 0   **D** 990

    B 10   **E** None of these

    C 90

16. $\dfrac{x}{5} = 10; x =$

    A $\dfrac{1}{2}$ **D** 50

    B 2   **E** None of these

    C 15

17. $4^3 4^6 =$

    A 4^9 **D** 16^{18}

    B 16^9 **E** None of these

    C 4^{18}

18. $4(3x^3 - 7) =$

    A $12x^3 - 7$ **D** $12x^{12} - 28$

    B $12x^7 - 7$ **E** None of these

    C $12x^3 - 28$

19. $4\frac{1}{5} \div 2\frac{1}{10}$

    A $\frac{1}{2}$ **D** $\frac{441}{50}$

    B 2 **E** None of these

    C $\frac{50}{441}$

20. $(.0004)(.004) =$

    A 1.6×10^{-8} **D** 1.6×10^{-5}

    B 1.6×10^{-7} **E** None of these

    C 1.6×10^{-6}

21. $^-5 - ^-5 - 5 =$

    A -15 **D** 5

    B -10 **E** None of these

    C -5

22. 3 is ___% of 5.

    A 20 **D** $166\frac{2}{3}$

    B 40 **E** None of these

    C 60

23. $1,000,000 =$

    A 10^6 D 10^{12}

    B 10^7 E None of these

    C 10^8

24. $\dfrac{24^4}{24^3}$

    A 1   D 48

    B $\dfrac{4}{3}$ E None of these

    C 24

25. $1\dfrac{4}{5} + 1\dfrac{1}{10} =$

    A $2\dfrac{5}{15}$ D $3\dfrac{9}{10}$

    B $2\dfrac{9}{10}$ E None of these

    C $3\dfrac{5}{15}$

26. 9% of 9 is

    A 0.01   D 81

    B 1   E None of these

    C 0.81

27. $3\dfrac{2}{3} \div 1\dfrac{2}{9} =$

    A $\dfrac{27}{121}$ D $\dfrac{121}{27}$

    B $\dfrac{1}{3}$ E None of these

    C 3

28. $3\frac{2}{3} \times 1\frac{2}{9} =$

     A $\frac{27}{121}$ **D** $\frac{121}{27}$

     B $\frac{1}{3}$ **E** None of these

     C 3

29. $3\frac{2}{3} + 1\frac{2}{9} =$

     A $4\frac{8}{9}$ **D** $4\frac{4}{12}$

     B $5\frac{8}{9}$ **E** None of these

     C $4\frac{6}{9}$

30. $3\frac{2}{3} - 1\frac{2}{9} =$

     A $2\frac{4}{9}$ **D** $1\frac{1}{6}$

     B $1\frac{4}{9}$ **E** None of these

     C $2\frac{1}{6}$

31. $0.01 - 0.001 =$

     A 0.011   **D** 0.099

     B 0.9   **E** None of these

     C 0.99

32. $4^3 - 4^2 - 4^1 - 4^0 =$

     A 0   **D** 46

     B 43   **E** None of these

     C 44

33. $\dfrac{-27}{27} =$

    A -1 **D** 54

    B 0   **E** None of these

    C 1

34. $x - 7 = -9; x =$

    A -16 **D** 16

    B -2 **E** None of these

    C 2

35. 50% of $\dfrac{1}{2} =$ _____

    A $\dfrac{1}{4}$ **D** 2

    B $\dfrac{1}{2}$ **E** None of these

    C 1

36. $\sqrt{3^2 + 4^2} =$

    A 5   **D** 12

    B 6   **E** None of these

    C 7

37. $4x + 5x - x =$

    A $-8x$ **D** $-20x^3$

    B $8x$ **E** None of these

    C $9x$

38. $3^{-2} =$

    A -9 **D** 9

    B $-\dfrac{1}{6}$ **E** None of these

    C $\dfrac{1}{9}$

39. $x + 14 = 14; x =$

     A 0   **D** 196

     B 1   **E** None of these

     C 28

40. $\dfrac{(\text{pig})^6}{(\text{pig})^3} =$

     A 2   **D** $(\text{pig})^3$

     B 3 pigs   **E** None of these

     C $(\text{pig})^2$

Part II: Applied Mathematics

Note *Calculators are permitted.*

1. Ulee goes 2 hours at 60 mph and 3 hours at 40 mph. His average speed in mph is

     A 45   **C** 50

     B 48   **D** 52

2. Simplify $5x + 7y - 2x$.

     A $7x + 7y$ **C** $-3x + 7y$

     B $3x + 7y$ **D** $-70x^2y$

3. A ten-sided polygon is a

     A Pentagon   **C** Decagon

     B Octagon   **D** Dodecagon

4. Vic bought a $400 item that was discounted 20% and then a 5% sales tax was added. Will bought a $400 item with 5% sales tax added first, and then the whole bill was discounted by 20%. Vic paid how much more than Will?

     A $40   **C** 0

     B $20   **D** $-$40

5. A $75 item is bought by Xavier for $56.25. The discount is

    A 15%   **C** 20%

    B $7\frac{1}{2}\%$ **D** 25%

For problems 6–12, use the two figures on the graph shown below.

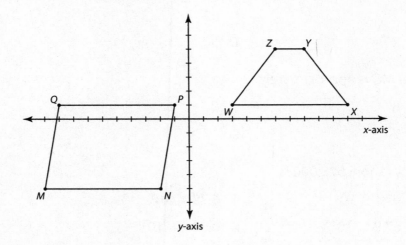

6. Figure *MNPQ* is a

    A Rectangle   **C** Rhombus

    B Parallelogram   **D** Trapezoid

7. Figure *WXYZ* is a

    A Rectangle   **C** Rhombus

    B Parallelogram   **D** Trapezoid

8. The area of *MNPQ* =

    A 24   **C** 48

    B 36   **D** 72

9. The area of *WXYZ* =

    A 14   **C** 18

    B 16   **D** 20

10. The length of $XY =$

    A 5   C 7

    B 6   D 8

11. The perimeter of *WXYZ* is

    A 16   C 24

    B 20   D 30

12. The length of *MQ* is approximately

    A 6   C 8

    B 7   D 37

13. In scientific notation, 678,000 is

    A 678×10^3 C 6.78×10^5

    B 67.8×10^4 D 0.678×10^6

14. An equilateral triangle with side 10 has a perimeter of

    A 30   C 60

    B 40   D $25\sqrt{3}$

15. If a triangle has angles 50°, 60°, and 70°, it is

    A Scalene   C Equilateral

    B Isosceles   D Obtuse

16. Yaz lost $20 when he sold an item. If he sold it for $50, his percentage loss was

    A 40%   C $28\frac{4}{7}\%$

    B $33\frac{1}{3}\%$ D 25%

17. $x^6 x^5 x =$

    A x^{11} C x^{30}

    B x^{12} D x^{7776}

18. $3y^0 + (3y)^0 =$

    A 1   C 4

    B 2   D $6y$

For problems 19–25, use the following roll totals if you throw 2 dice.

Roll of two dice	Ways to get that roll
2	1
3	2
4	3
5	4
6	5
7	6
8	5
9	4
10	3
11	2
12	1

19. The probability of rolling a 7 or 11 is

   A 8   **C** $\dfrac{2}{9}$

   B $\dfrac{2}{7}$ **D** $\dfrac{1}{3}$

20. The probability of rolling a 2, 3, or 12 is

   A $\dfrac{1}{2}$ **C** $\dfrac{1}{8}$

   B $\dfrac{1}{9}$ **D** $\dfrac{11}{6}$

21. Find the probability of rolling a number greater than 8.

   A $\dfrac{5}{6}$ **C** $\dfrac{5}{18}$

   B $\dfrac{5}{12}$ **D** $\dfrac{5}{36}$

22. Find the probability of rolling a number less than 4.

   A $\dfrac{1}{6}$ **C** $\dfrac{1}{12}$

   B $\dfrac{1}{9}$ **D** $\dfrac{1}{18}$

23. In how many ways can a sum of 2 or 7 be rolled?

   A 5   C 7

   B 6   D 8

24. In how many ways can a sum of 9, 10, or 11 be rolled?

   A 5   C 7

   B 6   D 9

25. The range is the largest number minus the smallest; the range of the results of the rolls is

   A 5   C 8

   B 7   D 10

26. 50% of $\frac{1}{2}$ of .5 of 800 is

   A 100   C 400

   B 200   D 800

27. $5x - 4x = 5; x =$

   A 0   C 4

   B 1   D 5

28. $-2x > 6$ is the same as

   A $x > -3$ C $x < -3$

   B $x \geq -3$ D $x \leq -3$

29. The volume of a cylinder is given as $\pi r^2 h$. If the diameter = height = 10 and $\pi = 3.14$, the volume is

   A 785   C 3140

   B 1570   D 6280

30. The legs of a right triangle are 9 and 40. The hypotenuse is

   A 41   C 45

   B 43   D 47

For problems 31–35, use the chart of grades presented below. The pie chart tells about the student population.

Total: 2000 Students

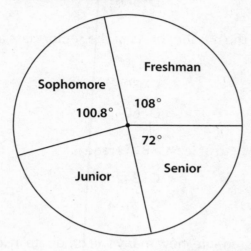

Average June 2010 grades

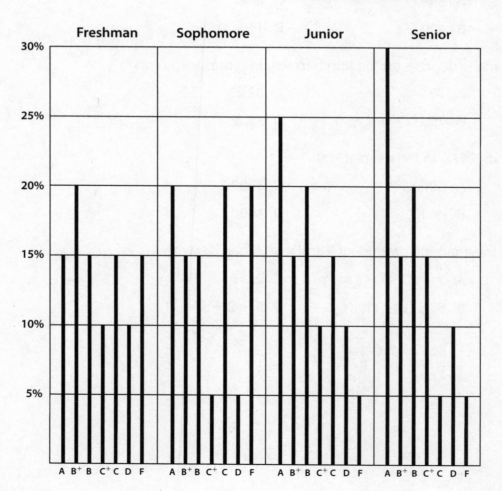

31. How many sophomores are there?

   A 500   C 550

   B 540   D 560

32. The difference between the number of A's of the senior class and the number of A's of the freshman class is

   A 9   C 30

   B 15   D 60

33. The number of students with at least a B average is

   A 225   C 842

   B 342   D 1104

34. If it takes at least a C to graduate, how many will graduate in 2010?

   A 340   C 842

   B 400   D 1584

35. How many degrees on the pie chart would represent juniors?

   A 70.2°   C 82.2°

   B 79.2°   D 99.2°

36. Round 4567.3 to the nearest 100.

   A 5000   C 5000.3

   B 4600   D 4600.3

37. "Five less than the product of 2 and x is 11" can be written

   A $2 + x - 5 = 11$ C $2x - 5 = 11$

   B $5 - 2x = 11$ D $5 - 2 - x = 11$

38. $a(b + c) = (b + c)a$ illustrates the

    A Commutative property of addition

    B Commutative property of multiplication

    C Distributive property of multiplication over addition

    D Associative property of multiplication

39. Zak gets a $124 bill for dinner and adds a 25% tip (probably not me). Zak pays

    A $149   **C** $165

    B $155   **D** $169

40. Sue has 3 $1 bills, 7 $2 bills, 8 $5 bills, and 7 $10 bills; how much money does Sue have?

    A $110   **C** $127

    B $117   **D** $142

For problems 41–45, use the following chart.

Trade of Country X with Country Y, 1997–2008 (U.S. dollars)

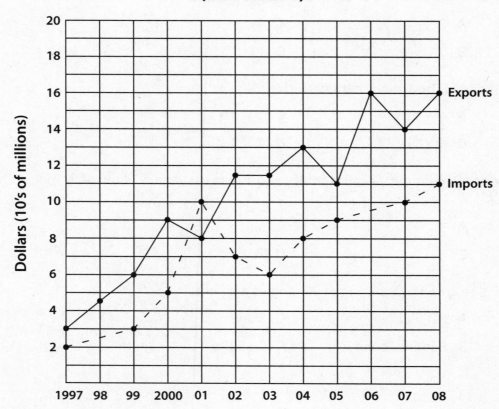

41. In 2003, exports are about what percentage of imports?

    A 5.5   C 53

    B 48   D 190

42. The largest percentage decrease in exports occurred from

    A 2000 to 2001   C 2004 to 2005

    B 2002 to 2003   D 2006 to 2007

43. The difference between the rise in imports from 2003 to 2004 and the rise in imports from 2004 to 2008 in millions of dollars is

    A 1   C 2

    B 1.5   D 10

44. In what year did the exports exceed the imports by the largest dollar amount?

    A 2001   C 2004

    B 2003   D 2006

45. How many years did the exports exceed the imports by more than $5 million?

    A 2   C 4

    B 3   D 11

46. 4 kilometers is how many centimeters?

    A 4×10^3 C 4×10^5

    B 4×10^4 D 4×10^6

47. Don walks 2 miles east, 4 miles south, and 1 mile east again. How many miles is he from home?

    A 3   C 5

    B 4   D 7

48. Two lines formed by meeting at 90° angles are called

    A Parallel   C Skew

    B Perpendicular   D Oblique

49. A $40 item is discounted 25%, followed by another 25% discount. Its final cost is

    A $17.50   **C** $22.50

    B $20   **D** $25

50. The minimum number of colors a cube can be colored without two faces of the same color touching is

    A 5   **C** 3

    B 4   **D** 2

Practice Test 4, Part I Answers

1. C: Line up the decimal points when you add.

2. C: $\frac{3}{6} + \frac{2}{6} + \frac{1}{6} = \frac{6}{6} = 1$.

3. D: $12 \times 12 = 144$.

4. D: Divide each side by 4.

5. B: $\frac{120}{.4} = \frac{1200}{4} = 300$.

6. C: A negative divided by a positive is negative.

7. A: $2 - 36 - 4 = -38$.

8. B: $2 - 2 = 0$.

9. D: $\frac{4}{10} = \frac{2}{5}$; only the 10 goes to the bottom.

10. C: 4 occurs the most.

11. C: The middle two numbers are 4 and 4; $\frac{4 + 4}{2} = 4$.

12. E: $\frac{3 + 4 + 4 + 3 + 4 + 12}{6} = \frac{30}{6} = 5$.

13. A: Multiply the tops and multiply the bottoms.

14. E: The answer is 0.047.

15. C: $100 - 10 = 90$.

16. D: Multiply each side by 5.

17. A: Add the exponents; the base stays the same.

18. C: Use the distribution property over subtraction.

19. B: $\frac{21}{5} \times \frac{10}{21} = \frac{10}{5} = 2$.

20. C: $4 \times 10^{-4} \times 4 \times 10^{-3} = 16 \times 10^{-7} = 1.6 \times 10^1 \times 10^{-7} = 1.6 \times 10^{-6}$.

21. C: $-5 + 5 - 5 = 0 - 5 = -5$.

22. C: $\frac{3}{5} = 60\%$.

23. A: It has 6 zeros, so 6 is the exponent.

24. C: Subtract exponents; base stays the same.

25. B: $1.8 + 1.1 = 2.9 = 2\frac{9}{10}$, or $\frac{9}{5} + \frac{11}{10} = \frac{18}{10} + \frac{11}{10} = \frac{29}{10} = 2\frac{9}{10}$.

26. C: $(.09)(9) = .81$.

27. C: $\frac{11}{3} \times \frac{9}{11} = \frac{9}{3} = 3$.

28. D: $\frac{11}{3} \times \frac{11}{9} = \frac{121}{27}$.

29. A: $3\frac{6}{9} + 1\frac{2}{9} = 4\frac{8}{9}$.

30. A: $3\frac{6}{9} - 1\frac{2}{9} = 2\frac{4}{9}$.

31. E: $.010 - .001 = .009$.

32. B: $64 - 16 - 4 - 1 = 43$.

33. A: A negative divided by a positive is negative.

34. B: Add 7 to each side.

35. A: $\frac{1}{2} \times \frac{1}{2} = \frac{1}{4}$; multiply tops and bottoms.

36. A: $\sqrt{9 + 16} = \sqrt{25} = 5$.

37. B: $4x + 5x - 1x = 9x - 1x = 8x$.

38. C: $\frac{1}{3^2} = \frac{1}{9}$.

39. A: Subtract 14 from each side.

40. D: Subtract exponents; base remains the same, no matter how crazy it may seem!

Practice Test 4, Part II Answers

1. B: Average speed $= \frac{\text{total distance}}{\text{total time}} \frac{2(60) + 3(40)}{5} = \frac{240}{5} = 48$.

2. C: $5x - 2x + 7y = 3x + 7y$

3. C: This is the definition of a *decagon*.

4. C: The order doesn't matter; you pay the same!

5. D: Percentage discount $= \frac{\text{discount}}{\text{total price}} \times 100\% = \frac{75 - 56.25}{75} \times 100\% = \frac{18.75}{.75} \times 100\% = 25\%$.

6. B: It has two pair of parallel sides.

7. D: It has only one pair of parallel sides.

8. C: $(8)(6) = 48$; count the boxes for the base and height; $b = 8$, $h = 6$.

9. D: Count the boxes for the height (4) and two bases (2 and 8). Then

   $A = \frac{1}{2}h(b_1 + b_2) = \frac{1}{2}(4)(2 + 8) = 20$.

10. A: It is the longest side of a $3-4-5$ Pythagorean triple.

11. B: *WZ* and *XY* are each 5; $5 + 5 + 2 + 8 = 20$.

12. A: This is the longest side of a right triangle with legs 2 and 6, $MQ = \sqrt{2^2 + 6^2} = \sqrt{40} \approx 6.32$.

13. C: Remember that the numerical part must be between 1 and 10. The decimal point is moved spaces to the left.

14. A: Equilateral means all sides are equal. $3 \times 10 = 30$.

15. A: All angles are unequal, so all sides are unequal. This is the definition of *scalene*.

16. C: Percentage loss $= \dfrac{\text{loss}}{\text{original price}} \times 100\% = \dfrac{20}{50 + 20} \times 100\% = \dfrac{20}{70} \times 100\% = 28\dfrac{4}{7}\%$.

17. B: When you multiply, add the exponents: $x^{6+5+1} = x^{12}$.

18. C: Anything to the 0 exponent is 1, so this is $3(1) + 1 = 4$.

19. C: The probability of a 7 or 11 $= Pr(7) + Pr(11) = \dfrac{6}{36} + \dfrac{2}{36} = \dfrac{8}{36} = \dfrac{2}{9}$.

20. B: $Pr(2, 3, \text{or } 12) = Pr(2) + Pr(3) + Pr(12) = \dfrac{1}{36} + \dfrac{2}{36} + \dfrac{1}{36} = \dfrac{4}{36} = \dfrac{1}{9}$.

21. C: $Pr(9) + Pr(10) + Pr(11) + Pr(12) = \dfrac{4 + 3 + 2 + 1}{36} = \dfrac{10}{36} = \dfrac{5}{18}$.

22. C: $Pr(2) + Pr(3) = \dfrac{1 + 2}{36} = \dfrac{3}{36} = \dfrac{1}{12}$.

23. C: $1 + 6$.

24. D: $4 + 3 + 2$

25. B: $12 - 2 = 10$

26. A. $\dfrac{1}{2}$ of $\dfrac{1}{2}$ of $\dfrac{1}{2}$ of 800 is $\dfrac{1}{2} \times \dfrac{1}{2} \times \dfrac{1}{2} \times 800 = 100$.

27. D: $5x - 4x = x$

28. C: When you divide an inequality by a negative, the order switches.

29. A: If $d = 10$, then $r = 5$, and $V = 3.14 \times 5 \times 5 \times 10 = 785$.

30. A: $c^2 = \sqrt{9^2 + 40^2} = \sqrt{81 + 1600} = \sqrt{1681} = 41$.

31. D: $\left(\dfrac{100.8}{360}\right)(2000) = 560$.

32. C: $\left(\dfrac{72}{360}\right)(2000) = 400$ seniors; $400(.30) = 120$ A's for seniors. $\left(\dfrac{108}{360}\right)(2000) = 600$

    freshmen; $600(.15) = 90$ A's for freshmen. $120 - 90 = 30$.

33. D: There are $2000 - 600 - 560 - 400 = 440$ juniors. At least a B: $.50(600) + .50(560) + .60(440) + .65(400) = 1104$.

34. A: $400(.85) = 340$. Only seniors graduate.

35. B: $360 - (100.8 + 108 + 72) = 79.2$.

36. B: You need to look only at the number to the right of the 100's place; it is 6, so round 4500 up 100 to 4600.

37. C: Remember, "less than" means to subtract the number.

38. B: Only the order of multiplication is changed; the numbers in the parentheses are not multiplied by a.

39. B: $\$124 + \left(\dfrac{1}{4}\right)(\$124) = \$124 + \$31 = \$155$.

40. C: $\$3 + \$14 + \$40 + \$70 = \$127$.

41. D: $\dfrac{\text{exports}}{\text{imports}} \times 100\% = \left(\dfrac{11.5}{6}\right)(100\%) \approx 190\%$. You can forget about the zeroes, and $\dfrac{11.5}{6}$ is a

    little less than 2. So you shouldn't have to actually do the arithmetic.

42. C: For 2004–2005 and 2006–2007, the drop is the same. However, the totals from 2004 to 2005 are smaller, so the percentage drop, which is approximately 15.4%, is higher for that period.

43. D: From 2003 to 2004, the rise is $8 - 6 = 2$ units; from 2004 to 2008, it is $11 - 8 = 3$ units. The difference is $3 - 2 = 1$ unit, where a unit is 10,000,000; so it is 10 millions of dollars.

44. D: Visually, it is 2006. $\$160$ million $- \$95$ million $= \$65$ million in 2006.

45. D: Because the chart is in tens of millions, 2001 is the only year it didn't happen.

46. C: Multiply by 1,000, and then by 100. 1 kilometer = 1000 meters, and 1 meter = 100 centimeters.

47. C: He has walked 3 miles east and 4 miles south. Again, this is a 3−4−5 Pythagorean triple.

48. B: This is the definition of *perpendicular*.

49. C: $\frac{1}{4}$ of $40 = $10; $40 − $10 = $30; $\frac{1}{4}$ of $30 = $7.50; $30 − $7.50 = $22.50.

50. C: Top and bottom one color, left and right another, and front and back a third color.

CHAPTER 14: *Epilogue*

"If you feel more is needed, you may need a little more for your confidence. But if our journey together has been complete, you have all you need for success."

Congratulations on finishing the book. Now you are ready to pass the math portion of the TABE Level A!!! When you do pass your TABE, I hope it brings you everything that you are hoping for.

Good luck in your career and the rest of your life!

Bob Miller

TABE *Level A*

ANSWER SHEETS

ANSWER SHEET: *Practice Test 1*

Part I: Mathematics Computation

1. Ⓐ Ⓑ Ⓒ Ⓓ Ⓔ
2. Ⓐ Ⓑ Ⓒ Ⓓ Ⓔ
3. Ⓐ Ⓑ Ⓒ Ⓓ Ⓔ
4. Ⓐ Ⓑ Ⓒ Ⓓ Ⓔ
5. Ⓐ Ⓑ Ⓒ Ⓓ Ⓔ
6. Ⓐ Ⓑ Ⓒ Ⓓ Ⓔ
7. Ⓐ Ⓑ Ⓒ Ⓓ Ⓔ
8. Ⓐ Ⓑ Ⓒ Ⓓ Ⓔ
9. Ⓐ Ⓑ Ⓒ Ⓓ Ⓔ
10. Ⓐ Ⓑ Ⓒ Ⓓ Ⓔ
11. Ⓐ Ⓑ Ⓒ Ⓓ Ⓔ
12. Ⓐ Ⓑ Ⓒ Ⓓ Ⓔ
13. Ⓐ Ⓑ Ⓒ Ⓓ Ⓔ
14. Ⓐ Ⓑ Ⓒ Ⓓ Ⓔ
15. Ⓐ Ⓑ Ⓒ Ⓓ Ⓔ
16. Ⓐ Ⓑ Ⓒ Ⓓ Ⓔ
17. Ⓐ Ⓑ Ⓒ Ⓓ Ⓔ
18. Ⓐ Ⓑ Ⓒ Ⓓ Ⓔ
19. Ⓐ Ⓑ Ⓒ Ⓓ Ⓔ
20. Ⓐ Ⓑ Ⓒ Ⓓ Ⓔ

21. Ⓐ Ⓑ Ⓒ Ⓓ Ⓔ
22. Ⓐ Ⓑ Ⓒ Ⓓ Ⓔ
23. Ⓐ Ⓑ Ⓒ Ⓓ Ⓔ
24. Ⓐ Ⓑ Ⓒ Ⓓ Ⓔ
25. Ⓐ Ⓑ Ⓒ Ⓓ Ⓔ
26. Ⓐ Ⓑ Ⓒ Ⓓ Ⓔ
27. Ⓐ Ⓑ Ⓒ Ⓓ Ⓔ
28. Ⓐ Ⓑ Ⓒ Ⓓ Ⓔ
29. Ⓐ Ⓑ Ⓒ Ⓓ Ⓔ
30. Ⓐ Ⓑ Ⓒ Ⓓ Ⓔ
31. Ⓐ Ⓑ Ⓒ Ⓓ Ⓔ
32. Ⓐ Ⓑ Ⓒ Ⓓ Ⓔ
33. Ⓐ Ⓑ Ⓒ Ⓓ Ⓔ
34. Ⓐ Ⓑ Ⓒ Ⓓ Ⓔ
35. Ⓐ Ⓑ Ⓒ Ⓓ Ⓔ
36. Ⓐ Ⓑ Ⓒ Ⓓ Ⓔ
37. Ⓐ Ⓑ Ⓒ Ⓓ Ⓔ
38. Ⓐ Ⓑ Ⓒ Ⓓ Ⓔ
39. Ⓐ Ⓑ Ⓒ Ⓓ Ⓔ
40. Ⓐ Ⓑ Ⓒ Ⓓ Ⓔ

Part II: Applied Mathematics

1. (A) (B) (C) (D)
2. (A) (B) (C) (D)
3. (A) (B) (C) (D)
4. (A) (B) (C) (D)
5. (A) (B) (C) (D)
6. (A) (B) (C) (D)
7. (A) (B) (C) (D)
8. (A) (B) (C) (D)
9. (A) (B) (C) (D)
10. (A) (B) (C) (D)
11. (A) (B) (C) (D)
12. (A) (B) (C) (D)
13. (A) (B) (C) (D)
14. (A) (B) (C) (D)
15. (A) (B) (C) (D)
16. (A) (B) (C) (D)
17. (A) (B) (C) (D)
18. (A) (B) (C) (D)
19. (A) (B) (C) (D)
20. (A) (B) (C) (D)
21. (A) (B) (C) (D)
22. (A) (B) (C) (D)
23. (A) (B) (C) (D)
24. (A) (B) (C) (D)
25. (A) (B) (C) (D)

26. (A) (B) (C) (D)
27. (A) (B) (C) (D)
28. (A) (B) (C) (D)
29. (A) (B) (C) (D)
30. (A) (B) (C) (D)
31. (A) (B) (C) (D)
32. (A) (B) (C) (D)
33. (A) (B) (C) (D)
34. (A) (B) (C) (D)
35. (A) (B) (C) (D)
36. (A) (B) (C) (D)
37. (A) (B) (C) (D)
38. (A) (B) (C) (D)
39. (A) (B) (C) (D)
40. (A) (B) (C) (D)
41. (A) (B) (C) (D)
42. (A) (B) (C) (D)
43. (A) (B) (C) (D)
44. (A) (B) (C) (D)
45. (A) (B) (C) (D)
46. (A) (B) (C) (D)
47. (A) (B) (C) (D)
48. (A) (B) (C) (D)
49. (A) (B) (C) (D)
50. (A) (B) (C) (D)

ANSWER SHEET: *Practice Test 2*

Part I: Mathematics Computation

1. (A) (B) (C) (D) (E)
2. (A) (B) (C) (D) (E)
3. (A) (B) (C) (D) (E)
4. (A) (B) (C) (D) (E)
5. (A) (B) (C) (D) (E)
6. (A) (B) (C) (D) (E)
7. (A) (B) (C) (D) (E)
8. (A) (B) (C) (D) (E)
9. (A) (B) (C) (D) (E)
10. (A) (B) (C) (D) (E)
11. (A) (B) (C) (D) (E)
12. (A) (B) (C) (D) (E)
13. (A) (B) (C) (D) (E)
14. (A) (B) (C) (D) (E)
15. (A) (B) (C) (D) (E)
16. (A) (B) (C) (D) (E)
17. (A) (B) (C) (D) (E)
18. (A) (B) (C) (D) (E)
19. (A) (B) (C) (D) (E)
20. (A) (B) (C) (D) (E)

21. (A) (B) (C) (D) (E)
22. (A) (B) (C) (D) (E)
23. (A) (B) (C) (D) (E)
24. (A) (B) (C) (D) (E)
25. (A) (B) (C) (D) (E)
26. (A) (B) (C) (D) (E)
27. (A) (B) (C) (D) (E)
28. (A) (B) (C) (D) (E)
29. (A) (B) (C) (D) (E)
30. (A) (B) (C) (D) (E)
31. (A) (B) (C) (D) (E)
32. (A) (B) (C) (D) (E)
33. (A) (B) (C) (D) (E)
34. (A) (B) (C) (D) (E)
35. (A) (B) (C) (D) (E)
36. (A) (B) (C) (D) (E)
37. (A) (B) (C) (D) (E)
38. (A) (B) (C) (D) (E)
39. (A) (B) (C) (D) (E)
40. (A) (B) (C) (D) (E)

Part II: Applied Mathematics

1. Ⓐ Ⓑ Ⓒ Ⓓ
2. Ⓐ Ⓑ Ⓒ Ⓓ
3. Ⓐ Ⓑ Ⓒ Ⓓ
4. Ⓐ Ⓑ Ⓒ Ⓓ
5. Ⓐ Ⓑ Ⓒ Ⓓ
6. Ⓐ Ⓑ Ⓒ Ⓓ
7. Ⓐ Ⓑ Ⓒ Ⓓ
8. Ⓐ Ⓑ Ⓒ Ⓓ
9. Ⓐ Ⓑ Ⓒ Ⓓ
10. Ⓐ Ⓑ Ⓒ Ⓓ
11. Ⓐ Ⓑ Ⓒ Ⓓ
12. Ⓐ Ⓑ Ⓒ Ⓓ
13. Ⓐ Ⓑ Ⓒ Ⓓ
14. Ⓐ Ⓑ Ⓒ Ⓓ
15. Ⓐ Ⓑ Ⓒ Ⓓ
16. Ⓐ Ⓑ Ⓒ Ⓓ
17. Ⓐ Ⓑ Ⓒ Ⓓ
18. Ⓐ Ⓑ Ⓒ Ⓓ
19. Ⓐ Ⓑ Ⓒ Ⓓ
20. Ⓐ Ⓑ Ⓒ Ⓓ
21. Ⓐ Ⓑ Ⓒ Ⓓ
22. Ⓐ Ⓑ Ⓒ Ⓓ
23. Ⓐ Ⓑ Ⓒ Ⓓ
24. Ⓐ Ⓑ Ⓒ Ⓓ
25. Ⓐ Ⓑ Ⓒ Ⓓ

26. Ⓐ Ⓑ Ⓒ Ⓓ
27. Ⓐ Ⓑ Ⓒ Ⓓ
28. Ⓐ Ⓑ Ⓒ Ⓓ
29. Ⓐ Ⓑ Ⓒ Ⓓ
30. Ⓐ Ⓑ Ⓒ Ⓓ
31. Ⓐ Ⓑ Ⓒ Ⓓ
32. Ⓐ Ⓑ Ⓒ Ⓓ
33. Ⓐ Ⓑ Ⓒ Ⓓ
34. Ⓐ Ⓑ Ⓒ Ⓓ
35. Ⓐ Ⓑ Ⓒ Ⓓ
36. Ⓐ Ⓑ Ⓒ Ⓓ
37. Ⓐ Ⓑ Ⓒ Ⓓ
38. Ⓐ Ⓑ Ⓒ Ⓓ
39. Ⓐ Ⓑ Ⓒ Ⓓ
40. Ⓐ Ⓑ Ⓒ Ⓓ
41. Ⓐ Ⓑ Ⓒ Ⓓ
42. Ⓐ Ⓑ Ⓒ Ⓓ
43. Ⓐ Ⓑ Ⓒ Ⓓ
44. Ⓐ Ⓑ Ⓒ Ⓓ
45. Ⓐ Ⓑ Ⓒ Ⓓ
46. Ⓐ Ⓑ Ⓒ Ⓓ
47. Ⓐ Ⓑ Ⓒ Ⓓ
48. Ⓐ Ⓑ Ⓒ Ⓓ
49. Ⓐ Ⓑ Ⓒ Ⓓ
50. Ⓐ Ⓑ Ⓒ Ⓓ

ANSWER SHEET: *Practice Test 3*

Part I: Mathematics Computation

1. Ⓐ Ⓑ Ⓒ Ⓓ Ⓔ
2. Ⓐ Ⓑ Ⓒ Ⓓ Ⓔ
3. Ⓐ Ⓑ Ⓒ Ⓓ Ⓔ
4. Ⓐ Ⓑ Ⓒ Ⓓ Ⓔ
5. Ⓐ Ⓑ Ⓒ Ⓓ Ⓔ
6. Ⓐ Ⓑ Ⓒ Ⓓ Ⓔ
7. Ⓐ Ⓑ Ⓒ Ⓓ Ⓔ
8. Ⓐ Ⓑ Ⓒ Ⓓ Ⓔ
9. Ⓐ Ⓑ Ⓒ Ⓓ Ⓔ
10. Ⓐ Ⓑ Ⓒ Ⓓ Ⓔ
11. Ⓐ Ⓑ Ⓒ Ⓓ Ⓔ
12. Ⓐ Ⓑ Ⓒ Ⓓ Ⓔ
13. Ⓐ Ⓑ Ⓒ Ⓓ Ⓔ
14. Ⓐ Ⓑ Ⓒ Ⓓ Ⓔ
15. Ⓐ Ⓑ Ⓒ Ⓓ Ⓔ
16. Ⓐ Ⓑ Ⓒ Ⓓ Ⓔ
17. Ⓐ Ⓑ Ⓒ Ⓓ Ⓔ
18. Ⓐ Ⓑ Ⓒ Ⓓ Ⓔ
19. Ⓐ Ⓑ Ⓒ Ⓓ Ⓔ
20. Ⓐ Ⓑ Ⓒ Ⓓ Ⓔ

21. Ⓐ Ⓑ Ⓒ Ⓓ Ⓔ
22. Ⓐ Ⓑ Ⓒ Ⓓ Ⓔ
23. Ⓐ Ⓑ Ⓒ Ⓓ Ⓔ
24. Ⓐ Ⓑ Ⓒ Ⓓ Ⓔ
25. Ⓐ Ⓑ Ⓒ Ⓓ Ⓔ
26. Ⓐ Ⓑ Ⓒ Ⓓ Ⓔ
27. Ⓐ Ⓑ Ⓒ Ⓓ Ⓔ
28. Ⓐ Ⓑ Ⓒ Ⓓ Ⓔ
29. Ⓐ Ⓑ Ⓒ Ⓓ Ⓔ
30. Ⓐ Ⓑ Ⓒ Ⓓ Ⓔ
31. Ⓐ Ⓑ Ⓒ Ⓓ Ⓔ
32. Ⓐ Ⓑ Ⓒ Ⓓ Ⓔ
33. Ⓐ Ⓑ Ⓒ Ⓓ Ⓔ
34. Ⓐ Ⓑ Ⓒ Ⓓ Ⓔ
35. Ⓐ Ⓑ Ⓒ Ⓓ Ⓔ
36. Ⓐ Ⓑ Ⓒ Ⓓ Ⓔ
37. Ⓐ Ⓑ Ⓒ Ⓓ Ⓔ
38. Ⓐ Ⓑ Ⓒ Ⓓ Ⓔ
39. Ⓐ Ⓑ Ⓒ Ⓓ Ⓔ
40. Ⓐ Ⓑ Ⓒ Ⓓ Ⓔ

Part II: Applied Mathematics

1. Ⓐ Ⓑ Ⓒ Ⓓ
2. Ⓐ Ⓑ Ⓒ Ⓓ
3. Ⓐ Ⓑ Ⓒ Ⓓ
4. Ⓐ Ⓑ Ⓒ Ⓓ
5. Ⓐ Ⓑ Ⓒ Ⓓ
6. Ⓐ Ⓑ Ⓒ Ⓓ
7. Ⓐ Ⓑ Ⓒ Ⓓ
8. Ⓐ Ⓑ Ⓒ Ⓓ
9. Ⓐ Ⓑ Ⓒ Ⓓ
10. Ⓐ Ⓑ Ⓒ Ⓓ
11. Ⓐ Ⓑ Ⓒ Ⓓ
12. Ⓐ Ⓑ Ⓒ Ⓓ
13. Ⓐ Ⓑ Ⓒ Ⓓ
14. Ⓐ Ⓑ Ⓒ Ⓓ
15. Ⓐ Ⓑ Ⓒ Ⓓ
16. Ⓐ Ⓑ Ⓒ Ⓓ
17. Ⓐ Ⓑ Ⓒ Ⓓ
18. Ⓐ Ⓑ Ⓒ Ⓓ
19. Ⓐ Ⓑ Ⓒ Ⓓ
20. Ⓐ Ⓑ Ⓒ Ⓓ
21. Ⓐ Ⓑ Ⓒ Ⓓ
22. Ⓐ Ⓑ Ⓒ Ⓓ
23. Ⓐ Ⓑ Ⓒ Ⓓ
24. Ⓐ Ⓑ Ⓒ Ⓓ
25. Ⓐ Ⓑ Ⓒ Ⓓ
26. Ⓐ Ⓑ Ⓒ Ⓓ
27. Ⓐ Ⓑ Ⓒ Ⓓ
28. Ⓐ Ⓑ Ⓒ Ⓓ
29. Ⓐ Ⓑ Ⓒ Ⓓ
30. Ⓐ Ⓑ Ⓒ Ⓓ
31. Ⓐ Ⓑ Ⓒ Ⓓ
32. Ⓐ Ⓑ Ⓒ Ⓓ
33. Ⓐ Ⓑ Ⓒ Ⓓ
34. Ⓐ Ⓑ Ⓒ Ⓓ
35. Ⓐ Ⓑ Ⓒ Ⓓ
36. Ⓐ Ⓑ Ⓒ Ⓓ
37. Ⓐ Ⓑ Ⓒ Ⓓ
38. Ⓐ Ⓑ Ⓒ Ⓓ
39. Ⓐ Ⓑ Ⓒ Ⓓ
40. Ⓐ Ⓑ Ⓒ Ⓓ
41. Ⓐ Ⓑ Ⓒ Ⓓ
42. Ⓐ Ⓑ Ⓒ Ⓓ
43. Ⓐ Ⓑ Ⓒ Ⓓ
44. Ⓐ Ⓑ Ⓒ Ⓓ
45. Ⓐ Ⓑ Ⓒ Ⓓ
46. Ⓐ Ⓑ Ⓒ Ⓓ
47. Ⓐ Ⓑ Ⓒ Ⓓ
48. Ⓐ Ⓑ Ⓒ Ⓓ
49. Ⓐ Ⓑ Ⓒ Ⓓ
50. Ⓐ Ⓑ Ⓒ Ⓓ

ANSWER SHEET: *Practice Test 4*

Part I: Mathematics Computation

1. A B C D E
2. A B C D E
3. A B C D E
4. A B C D E
5. A B C D E
6. A B C D E
7. A B C D E
8. A B C D E
9. A B C D E
10. A B C D E
11. A B C D E
12. A B C D E
13. A B C D E
14. A B C D E
15. A B C D E
16. A B C D E
17. A B C D E
18. A B C D E
19. A B C D E
20. A B C D E
21. A B C D E
22. A B C D E
23. A B C D E
24. A B C D E
25. A B C D E
26. A B C D E
27. A B C D E
28. A B C D E
29. A B C D E
30. A B C D E
31. A B C D E
32. A B C D E
33. A B C D E
34. A B C D E
35. A B C D E
36. A B C D E
37. A B C D E
38. A B C D E
39. A B C D E
40. A B C D E

Part II: Applied Mathematics

1. Ⓐ Ⓑ Ⓒ Ⓓ
2. Ⓐ Ⓑ Ⓒ Ⓓ
3. Ⓐ Ⓑ Ⓒ Ⓓ
4. Ⓐ Ⓑ Ⓒ Ⓓ
5. Ⓐ Ⓑ Ⓒ Ⓓ
6. Ⓐ Ⓑ Ⓒ Ⓓ
7. Ⓐ Ⓑ Ⓒ Ⓓ
8. Ⓐ Ⓑ Ⓒ Ⓓ
9. Ⓐ Ⓑ Ⓒ Ⓓ
10. Ⓐ Ⓑ Ⓒ Ⓓ
11. Ⓐ Ⓑ Ⓒ Ⓓ
12. Ⓐ Ⓑ Ⓒ Ⓓ
13. Ⓐ Ⓑ Ⓒ Ⓓ
14. Ⓐ Ⓑ Ⓒ Ⓓ
15. Ⓐ Ⓑ Ⓒ Ⓓ
16. Ⓐ Ⓑ Ⓒ Ⓓ
17. Ⓐ Ⓑ Ⓒ Ⓓ
18. Ⓐ Ⓑ Ⓒ Ⓓ
19. Ⓐ Ⓑ Ⓒ Ⓓ
20. Ⓐ Ⓑ Ⓒ Ⓓ
21. Ⓐ Ⓑ Ⓒ Ⓓ
22. Ⓐ Ⓑ Ⓒ Ⓓ
23. Ⓐ Ⓑ Ⓒ Ⓓ
24. Ⓐ Ⓑ Ⓒ Ⓓ
25. Ⓐ Ⓑ Ⓒ Ⓓ

26. Ⓐ Ⓑ Ⓒ Ⓓ
27. Ⓐ Ⓑ Ⓒ Ⓓ
28. Ⓐ Ⓑ Ⓒ Ⓓ
29. Ⓐ Ⓑ Ⓒ Ⓓ
30. Ⓐ Ⓑ Ⓒ Ⓓ
31. Ⓐ Ⓑ Ⓒ Ⓓ
32. Ⓐ Ⓑ Ⓒ Ⓓ
33. Ⓐ Ⓑ Ⓒ Ⓓ
34. Ⓐ Ⓑ Ⓒ Ⓓ
35. Ⓐ Ⓑ Ⓒ Ⓓ
36. Ⓐ Ⓑ Ⓒ Ⓓ
37. Ⓐ Ⓑ Ⓒ Ⓓ
38. Ⓐ Ⓑ Ⓒ Ⓓ
39. Ⓐ Ⓑ Ⓒ Ⓓ
40. Ⓐ Ⓑ Ⓒ Ⓓ
41. Ⓐ Ⓑ Ⓒ Ⓓ
42. Ⓐ Ⓑ Ⓒ Ⓓ
43. Ⓐ Ⓑ Ⓒ Ⓓ
44. Ⓐ Ⓑ Ⓒ Ⓓ
45. Ⓐ Ⓑ Ⓒ Ⓓ
46. Ⓐ Ⓑ Ⓒ Ⓓ
47. Ⓐ Ⓑ Ⓒ Ⓓ
48. Ⓐ Ⓑ Ⓒ Ⓓ
49. Ⓐ Ⓑ Ⓒ Ⓓ
50. Ⓐ Ⓑ Ⓒ Ⓓ

Part III: Applied Mathematics

TABE *Level A*

INDEX

INDEX

MAY - 2017

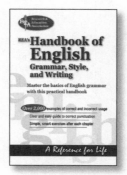

REA's Test Preps
The Best in Test Preparation

- REA "Test Preps" are **far more** comprehensive than any other test preparation series
- Each book contains full-length practice tests based on the most recent exams
- **Every** type of question likely to be given on the exams is included
- Answers are accompanied by **full** and **detailed** explanations

REA publishes hundreds of test prep books. Some of our titles include:

Advanced Placement Exams (APs)
Art History
Biology
Calculus AB & BC
Chemistry
Economics
English Language & Composition
English Literature & Composition
European History
French Language
Government & Politics
Latin Vergil
Physics B & C
Psychology
Spanish Language
Statistics
United States History
World History

College-Level Examination Program (CLEP)
American Government
College Algebra
General Examinations
History of the United States I
History of the United States II
Introduction to Educational Psychology
Human Growth and Development
Introductory Psychology
Introductory Sociology
Principles of Management
Principles of Marketing
Spanish
Western Civilization I
Western Civilization II

SAT Subject Tests
Biology E/M
Chemistry
French
German
Literature
Mathematics Level 1, 2
Physics
Spanish
United States History

Graduate Record Exams (GREs)
Biology
Chemistry
Computer Science
General
Literature in English
Mathematics
Physics
Psychology

ACT - ACT Assessment

ASVAB - Armed Services Vocational Aptitude Battery

CBEST - California Basic Educational Skills Test

CDL - Commercial Driver License Exam

CLAST - College Level Academic Skills Test

COOP, HSPT & TACHS - Catholic High School Admission Tests

FE (EIT) - Fundamentals of Engineering Exams

FTCE - Florida Teacher Certification Examinations

GED

GMAT - Graduate Management Admission Test

LSAT - Law School Admission Test

MAT - Miller Analogies Test

MCAT - Medical College Admission Test

MTEL - Massachusetts Tests for Educator Licensure

NJ HSPA - New Jersey High School Proficiency Assessment

NYSTCE - New York State Teacher Certification Examinations

PRAXIS PLT - Principles of Learning & Teaching Tests

PRAXIS PPST - Pre-Professional Skills Tests

PSAT/NMSQT

SAT

TExES - Texas Examinations of Educator Standards

THEA - Texas Higher Education Assessment

TOEFL - Test of English as a Foreign Language

USMLE Steps 1,2,3 - U.S. Medical Licensing Exams

For information about any of REA's books, visit www.rea.com

Research & Education Association
61 Ethel Road W., Piscataway, NJ 08854
Phone: (732) 819-8880